Core Themes

Core Themes

Discover Your Path

to a Purpose-Driven

Career

Raymond A. Inglesi, M.A.

CUSTOM COMMUNICATIONS
PUBLISHER
Biddeford, Maine

Core Themes: Discover Your Path to a Purpose-Driven Career

Published by Custom Communications, Inc.
11 Wentworth Street, Biddeford, ME 04005
www.desktoppub.com

Core Themes

Raymond A. Inglesi, M.A.
Fifty Portland Pier, Suite 300
Portland, ME 04101
(866) 353-3523
e-mail: ringlesi@corethemes.com
http://www.corethemes.com

Library of Congress Control Number: 2012930174

ISBN-13: 978-1-892168-16-0

Book design: Custom Communications, Inc.

Artwork: © 2012 Donna Stackhouse

Dust jacket design: delaney-designs.com

Author photograph: Dan Lambert

1 3 5 6 4 2

For my Core Themes clients

CONTENTS

Core
Themes

Foreword

There is an epidemic of bright, accomplished, good people who dread going to work each day. You may have a vague feeling that your life's work is not what you intended, not satisfying enough, or fun enough, or important enough to yourself or the world. Do you have to force yourself to walk through those impressive glass doors every morning into a highly regarded profession you have grown to hate? Is your job making you physically sick or emotionally dead to your loved ones?

Life is short, and it is far too precious to waste that way. Instead of gritting your teeth and counting the days to retirement, you can spend your time—and earn your living—doing what delights you. You can bound out of bed because you can't wait to see what discoveries the day may bring.

Work can be that way. It should be that way.

Making big changes in your life's work takes courage. It also requires a good plan, contemplation, and a realistic assessment of who you are, what matters most to you, and what you love (and hate) to do.

What exactly do you want to do with your life? In wrestling with this all-important question, you have to answer an equally important question—what am I going to do with my time?

Identifying your Core Themes is the first step toward answering these questions. The Core Themes program provides a proven and rational method for seeing yourself as you really are. That self-knowledge will give you the tools to build a career that brings satisfaction instead of boredom. It will lead you to a state of harmony between your personal and professional self.

You can make the choice to be fulfilled, to follow your dreams. This book is a call to action for you to take control of your career, your life, and your happiness. If you follow your Core Themes, you will find real fulfillment and meaning every day of your life.

INTRODUCTION

Go confidently in the direction of your dreams!
Live the life you've imagined.

—Henry David Thoreau

In the early 1990s I first introduced clients in my career consulting business to Core Themes, those unique and strongly held values, needs, and interests that define each of us personally and professionally. As I guided my clients toward identifying their own unique Core Themes and showed them how to follow their dreams to the right career, I often witnessed amazing transformations begin to take place.

When Alicia, a bright, twenty-five-year-old Ivy League graduate, came to my office, she was unhappy in her current job and confused about what to do next. After going through the Core Themes program, she accepted a position with a well-known charitable foundation aiding children and families in Africa, a job that has become her life's passion.

Todd, a successful school administrator, was a prime candidate for a heart attack when he arrived for his first appointment. Overweight and under constant stress, Todd dreaded the school board meetings his job required. As we worked together on his Core Themes journey, Todd discovered a different career path as a human resources director that has brought him satisfaction and fulfillment—without the hated meetings. He also lost weight, lowered his cholesterol, and is a much happier person today.

After years of commuting two hours a day with little time for her husband and two young children, Emily was ready to find work that could bring greater balance to her life. But she had no idea what she could do or where she should look for a new job. During the course of her Core Themes work, Emily was able to redefine what she wanted in life and a career and the conditions that were important to her. After exploring opportunities using her Core Themes as a guide, she found the ideal job five minutes from her home. Most important, she can now see her children off to school in the morning and be there when the bus arrives in the afternoon. No more nanny!

Daniel, a controller for a successful insurance company, turned to the Core Themes program after he failed to win the chief financial officer position in his company. What he discovered surprised him. After identifying the aspects of life he valued most, he left his profession and accepted a position as director of a nonprofit organization dedicated to working with families experiencing extreme poverty. This critical change in his life and career brought him the personal, professional, and spiritual fulfillment he needed for inner peace.

What these people have in common—besides successful careers—is a commitment to their Core Themes. They have accepted the fact that to be truly happy, they must incorporate their Core Themes into any career they pursue.

After two decades of honing the Core Themes methodology and helping clients find true purpose and meaning in their lives, I realized that many others could benefit from Core Themes. As you read this book, you may recognize elements of yourself in the real-life stories of people who were stuck in unrewarding jobs, yet found the way to fulfillment.

Ultimately, this book intends to inspire
 • those of you who feel frozen in unsatisfying careers, trapped in boring occupations because of the paycheck they provide, or who stay in dead-end jobs, paralyzed by an overwhelming fear of change;

- those soon-to-be college graduates and recent graduates who want to discover their true career direction;
- anyone wishing to reach a higher level of personal and professional satisfaction; and
- counselors and other professionals seeking a better way to help their clients gain clarity and purpose in their lives and careers.

Core Themes provides a proven and rational method for seeing yourself as you really are. If you're feeling trapped in your work or confused about your career direction, a Core Themes-trained professional can help you find your way. If there isn't one nearby, you'll find in Chapter 10 the information you need to interview counselors and find one whose approach may help you along the path.

If you're a helping professional, this book will demonstrate the power of the Core Themes methodology. I hope you will be inspired to pursue the Core Themes training and certification. Chapter 11 explains more about this.

My sincere hope for both the help-seekers and help-givers is that you will be inspired to pursue a new way of finding harmony between the personal and the professional self.

Important Concepts

Change A critical element in developing your Core Themes is freeing yourself from beliefs and notions that no longer work for you. By changing your mind-set, you can make decisions about your life and career in a more enlightened way.

Choice You are where you are because you made choices along the way to get there. Now it's time to make better choices about your life and career.

Clarity You need to be able to think about and see clearly the range of possibilities open to you. It is difficult to navigate accurately if clutter obscures the way.

Clutter A messy chorus of rationalizations (clutter) can lock you in place. Too much clutter and you'll be *stuck*.

Getting to Know You The better you know yourself, the better the decisions you are able to make in your life and career. It's time for some serious reflection.

Life Is Short It's amazing how time goes by so quickly. If you keep postponing things, you may find that you have run out of time. Take those important steps now.

Personal Responsibility There is only one person responsible for your life and the decisions you make—the person you see in the mirror. The sooner you accept this concept, the sooner you will begin to make the changes that lead to a happier and more productive life and career.

Work Because you spend most of your waking moments at work, you owe it to yourself to be relentless in finding a career that is fulfilling and meaningful to you.

ONE

Work and Happiness—
The Good News

Your work is going to fill a large part of your life, and the only way to be truly satisfied is to do what you believe is great work. And the only way to do great work is to love what you do. If you haven't found it yet, keep looking. Don't settle. As with all matters of the heart, you'll know when you find it. And, like any great relationship, it just gets better as the years roll on.

—Steve Jobs (Apple founder to Stanford grads)

This book is for people who want to enjoy going to work again.

It's for the teacher who is tired and unenthusiastic in his job of fifteen years but can't imagine a way out.

It's for the vice president of marketing who, at age forty and with two small children at home, has grown to hate the travel, deadlines, and long hours that her job requires yet is paralyzed by the prospect of replacing her six-figure income or living with less.

It's for the middle-aged surgeon who has spent fourteen years building a successful practice but now can hardly bear the thought of the schedule of surgeries ahead of him and who realizes that the only thing he likes about his work is the money it generates.

It's for the recent graduate seeking a career path that is focused and purposeful. It is for the young person who is looking for real meaning in a world of constant change and uncertainty.

It's for the Baby Boomers and soon-to-be retirees who will dominate the demographics in the next decade. These folks have a unique challenge ahead of them—how to fill the remaining years of their life with worthwhile pursuits.

It's for the individual who has been out of the work force for a period of time and is now considering another career direction, but what?

This book is for anyone who is struggling to be satisfied with that massive piece of our lives called work. It's about overcoming unhappiness and finding fulfillment, not just by changing companies or jobs but by figuring out what we truly want to do with our lives, then developing a course of action to achieve it. It can be done, but it takes determination and courage. This book will show you how.

I see fresh evidence every day of how people filled with frustration, sadness, anger, uncertainty, and worry over their chosen careers can and do reinvent themselves. This book is based on my thirty-eight years of professional experience— the first twelve years as a psychotherapist, the last twenty-six consulting to businesses (profit and nonprofit) across the country on the various "people issues" that impact productivity and performance. It is based on observations of real people over time—what troubles them, what keeps them from having satisfying jobs, and what can be done to make their lives better.

It is about getting unstuck. It is about discovering your unique purpose and meaning in life.

THE POSSIBILITIES

Through the years I have witnessed amazing success stories of clients who followed their dreams. Many came to my office confused and unhappy over their career situations. The Core Themes program helped them identify the important elements of their lives: their core values, goals, and passions. Armed with that knowledge, they were able to seek and find career paths that matched their inner nature and helped them achieve their life's purpose. Here are three inspiring accounts of clients who found careers that have brought them fulfillment and happiness.

SUCCESS #1: ALICIA'S STORY

Dear Mom & Dad, guess where I'm going? Africa!

Alicia completed the Core Themes program two and a half years after graduating from college. After spending several months exploring opportunities that would complement her Core Themes, she accepted a position with a well-known international health foundation and in the spring of 2008 headed off to Nigeria.

We began our work in early 2007 when Alicia, at her father's suggestion, asked me to help her sort out her career path. At the young age of twenty-five, Alicia had already accumulated an impressive list of credentials. She graduated summa cum laude from Dartmouth College with a B.A. in biology (with a focus on neurobiology); received high honors in her major for her thesis and honors from several prestigious organizations, including the Phi Beta Kappa Society, the Key Honor Society, and the National Society of Collegiate Scholars; and was named a recipient of a Waterhouse Research Grant.

An accomplished equestrian, Alicia competed in the Junior Olympics and was the youngest instructor to become certified by the U.S. Dressage Federation. She also had traveled to a number of countries including South Africa, Tanzania, Spain, Italy, the Netherlands, and Germany.

When Alicia came to see me, she was sure of one thing, that she did not want to spend her life working in a laboratory doing research. "I love lab research and what it could do to make a difference in people's lives," she told me, "but I don't like the day-to-day lab work."

As we began the Core Themes program, our key goal was to help Alicia focus clearly on her career options. This turned out to be a daunting task because Alicia had a number of possibilities to consider: psychology, public health, education, teaching, FBI/CIA, think tanks, international development, dressage, consulting, research, neuroscience, and medicine.

A mature young woman, Alicia had a cultured background, academic credentials, and a common-sense attitude—all of which presented her with many choices. However, Alicia had one fairly serious complication that needed to be considered regardless of her final decision. As a teenager, Alicia had been diagnosed with Chronic Fatigue Syndrome (CFS). She had learned to manage her health reasonably well, but the condition occasionally forced her to stay in bed for days at a time.

To Alicia's credit, she never allowed CFS to control her life or her activities. Her commitment to the Core Themes process was unwavering, despite a few challenging periods. Certainly, Alicia's health had to be a consideration in her career decision, but once she made a commitment, there was no stopping her.

As we progressed through Phase 1 of the process, Alicia's personal history provided important clues to her personality and values. Alicia grew up in a loving and supportive home, with successful, intelligent parents. This environment was nurturing, but her parents' success also caused Alicia to put pressure on herself to be successful. "I don't do well with not doing well," Alicia acknowledged.

As part of Phase 1, Alicia took a battery of tests, questionnaires, and surveys designed to examine her personality, abilities and aptitudes, skills, motivations, interests, values, communication style, and emotional intelligence. The tests showed that Alicia had superior analytical skills and an exceptional ability to think conceptually. Her verbal comprehension and mathematical aptitude were well above average.

On the personal side, the findings identified her as a strong feeler and thinker. She had a real concern for others and wanted to make a difference in people's lives. This quality turned out to be one of Alicia's main Core Themes, an important one that ultimately influenced her choice of careers.

Alicia's high analytical ability led her to examine the facts and other relevant data carefully before making any important decisions in her life. At times this caused her to "overthink" situations and made it difficult for her to reach a decision. Further analysis of the test data showed that Alicia had several strong needs:

- a desire to achieve and accomplish important things

- a take-charge attitude and a willingness to initiate action
- a powerful need to experience change and variety
- a strong need to be recognized for accomplishments

Other test results identified more traits in Alicia:
- a fine-tuned sensitivity to other people, which made her agreeable and accommodating with an ability to develop long-term relationships
- an extremely conscientious nature that made her dependable and likely to abide by the rules
- a strong desire to serve others and improve society
- a desire to have frequent and varied contact with other people
- a tendency to be diligent and a perfectionist
- an eagerness to please and work with others collaboratively
- a strong interest in aesthetics and design
- an interest in science and technology

Alicia exhibited little interest in commerce, earning money, or business. As we progressed through the next steps, Alicia gained more insight and understanding of herself. She began to understand what mattered most to her and what she wanted to do with her life. Her responses were insightful and prophetic. "I like to educate people." "I like to inspire people to help themselves." "I'm interested in doing something unique, something others aren't able to do." "I want to be the best that I can be." "I want to make people's lives better by increasing knowledge that helps people solve problems." "My goal is to participate in some large cause that is essential for people's happiness."

Within several months Alicia's hard work as she progressed through the program enabled her to identify the Core Themes that she required in a career:

- learning and intellectual stimulation
- variety, novelty, and ongoing change
- an opportunity to become an expert in a profession
- a focus on a worthwhile cause and on helping people
- the ability to play a leadership role
- an environment that encourages sharing and collaborating with colleagues
- a great deal of autonomy on the job

In the final phase of the process, Alicia explored various opportunities, gathered valuable information, and met with former professors and others engaged in areas of interest to her to find a career that fulfilled her Core Themes. After several months of exploring, she accepted an exciting offer, a volunteer position with the William J. Clinton Foundation focused on strengthening pediatric HIV/AIDS care and treatment in Nigeria.

In the summer of 2008, Alicia flew across an ocean to delve into a program providing essential medicines and technical assistance to improve the lives of the neediest children in Nigeria. Her position evolved into a full-time role as operations director, through which she gained valuable experience in all aspects of the program. Only a year after arriving in Nigeria, Alicia accepted a promotion to a position in Swaziland.

Alicia is now country manager for the Clinton Health Access Initiative in Swaziland, which provides essential commodities and key technical assistance to the Ministry of Health to strengthen HIV/AIDS care and treatment and to support an initiative aimed at eliminating malaria in the African nation.

In deciding to accept the position with the Clinton Foundation, Alicia chose to leave her comfortable lifestyle in Boston, her loving family, a boyfriend, and all she had grown to know and love for a cause that she felt passionate about and believed in with all her heart. That decision was a difficult one on many fronts, but it has brought her great satisfaction and happiness in both her work and her life.

Amazingly, her new career choice has provided Alicia an opportunity to realize nearly all of her Core Themes. Alicia confided that this is one of the first times in her life she has felt truly content and is not worrying about the future and where she is going to be in five years. She is living in the moment, yet moving forward in a meaningful way, continuing to grow and develop.

And her family and friends say that Alicia has never looked happier.

Success #2: David's Story

David attended a Catholic university because his mother told him, "I don't care what college you attend, as long as it is a Catholic one." So David went to Fordham University and four years later graduated with a degree in history. He had no real reason for pursing the major other than an interest in history and a lack of interest in any other field. From the age of twelve, David had made decisions based on his desire to be accepted by his peers, rather than developing his own thoughts, interests, abilities, and feelings. "I felt like I stopped being authentic," David confided during his Core Themes sessions. "Just being myself was not enough."

Fast forward to the present. At age forty-three, David

found himself trapped in a job which offered him little fulfillment or happiness. On the surface, David had achieved the
American dream—financial success, professional advance-
ment, a lovely wife, and supportive parents. Inside, however,
David felt "stuck" in a job that was extracting a physical
and emotional toll. For years he had shelved his own dreams
and accepted a skewed view of himself as a man with medio-
cre capabilities who tied his self-worth to the ability to earn
money and to please others.

David began his Core Themes work with a good measure of skepticism that it could lead to real and lasting change.
He gave all the usual excuses ("clutter") for not being able
to walk away from an unsatisfying job: he had to pay the
mortgage; other people—his wife, his parents—might think
badly of him; he didn't have the intelligence or the skill to
work at anything else. What drove David to complete the
course was the certain knowledge that he was unhappy and
had been for many years. It wasn't simply a bad boss or not
liking the company's policies or not earning enough money
or too much travel. Whatever lay at the root of his discontent
was much more serious, and David knew it.

"Something is missing but I don't know what," David
said at his first session. "All I know is that I am unhappy and
have no sense of purpose in my career."

David's physical symptoms were fairly obvious: he had
stopped exercising and had gained weight and complained of
backache, tense muscles, and other woes.

Early in the process David had a "breakthrough" when
the test scores revealed that he had the cognitive ability to
achieve success in many areas. The results showed him to be
far above average in both analytical and conceptual thinking when compared to a group of top executives. Until then,

David had believed that he was not intelligent, a belief that had enabled him to avoid taking risks or challenging himself. This strategy assured that he would never fail.

After about an hour or so, David finally acknowledged that he was more intelligent than he had let on. Of course, this also meant that he could no longer hide behind the excuse of not being intelligent.

As he progressed through the program, David gained more confidence that something positive was going to come from his hard work. Although he was still working in a job that provided little personal reward, he wasn't quite ready to leave the good salary it provided.

After several drafts, David seemed confident with his Core Themes list. One of the top Core Themes on his list, not surprising, was his need to be involved in situations, problem-solving activities, or solutions that required thought, analysis, research, and observation. This allowed him to exercise his high analytical and conceptual abilities.

Several of David's other Core Themes included

Integrity. To David, integrity meant that the motivation to do his job came from within—the belief that what he was doing made a difference in his life and the lives of others. David needed a job where he truly knew what he was talking about and could be open and honest about his services, the products he sold, and the way the work was accomplished.

Autonomy. David needed to have control over his work environment, his schedule, and the way he performed his job. He wanted to have a leadership role in planning strategy and making decisions about his work.

Family and Personal Life Balance. David valued his home life and yearned for a job that allowed him to spend more time with his wife, his family, his friends, and his dogs.

He wanted to devote the time necessary to develop a nurturing and loving relationship with his wife.

Compassion. David wanted to help others choose a direction in their life or make difficult decisions that were important to them.

David made his own important decision shortly after "discovering" his Core Themes; he resigned from his job. In the next few months he pursued job opportunities using his Core Themes as a guide and a new, improved resume. During job interviews, David discussed his Core Themes and their importance in his life. His open and deliberate approach to finding work impressed several interviewers.

Success came when David accepted a job that met nearly all the requirements of his Core Themes. He's now in a job he loves—a position with a company that develops and markets health care products to women satisfies his need to make a positive difference in people's lives. Additionally, David is able to use his intellectual abilities more fully as he draws from his analytical and conceptual skills to help direct product development.

"What's important to me now," he said, "is that I'm happy in what I'm doing. I now know that if I'm happy in what I'm doing, everything else is going to be fine." David cleared away his clutter and faced his fears and is now in a much better place. He is happier, healthier, and living his Core Themes.

Success #3: Emily's Story

After eighteen years of working for a world-class retailer, Emily decided she was ready to embark on a different career. But what? Answering that question would be the focus of our Core Themes work together.

Emily, an expert in retail business, had extensive experience in identifying and overseeing the purchase of products that customers wanted to buy. She was especially good at managing and motivating people. In spite of her obvious success and acquired skills and experience, Emily felt that something was missing in her career. Like many of my clients, Emily could not say what was missing.

We began our Core Themes work by examining in great detail Emily's personal background and professional experiences. A competitive person by nature, she always strived to do her best and took on the lion's share of the responsibilities in whatever she pursued. During her four years at college, Emily worked summers for an outdoor amusement park. Her boss soon put her in charge of running the business full time during the summer. She loved the park job, where she hired the young staff, learned to troubleshoot problems, and got firsthand experience in managing. She also learned something about herself—that she loved the autonomy and the entrepreneurial spirit of a business environment.

After graduating with a B.S. degree in biopsychology, Emily accepted a position with a major retailer, where she progressed through the ranks. Her professional experiences included managing projects, running operations, and overseeing the purchasing of products as well as serving a prominent role in the business's leadership. She learned a great deal and for many years enjoyed her broad business experiences.

To learn more about her skills and personality, Emily underwent a number of tests. I also conducted an in-depth examination of her personal history. The results of the career testing shed light on Emily's strengths, cognitive abilities, motivations, and interests. Emily tested high in her ability to analyze problems, visualize solutions, reason, and communicate with other people. These findings suggested that whatever she chose to do in her career, she needed to be challenged and have opportunities to practice these strong skills.

Emily's personal history revealed that she is a take-charge person with a high level of energy, competitive, and self-sufficient. A no-nonsense woman, she likes to be active and to act decisively. As an outgoing person, she tends to be expressive and demonstrative when engaging with others. At the same time, her sensitive nature can cause her to feel anxious. The tests also showed that Emily has a strong desire to achieve, a need for autonomy, an even stronger need to take charge, and a need for variety and change. She is not shy about challenging others.

By exploring her strengths and character traits through the tests and personal history, Emily began to see what was really important to her. It wasn't having a fancy title or making a lot of money or climbing the corporate ladder. She discovered after a great deal of discussion and reflection that what she valued the most was having a life that was balanced between her personal time (with its responsibilities as a mother and a wife) and a career that was challenging and fulfilling.

The career she sought also had to be intellectually stimulating, provide a large measure of independence, enable her to act decisively when necessary, and offer her continued opportunities for professional growth. All of this and a balanced lifestyle, too!

With her newfound knowledge and armed with her Core Themes, Emily set out to discover the opportunities that would fulfill her objectives. After some diligent networking, she met two entrepreneurs who, impressed with Emily's qualifications, created a position for her in their company.

Emily negotiated a deal that allows her to start her business day after she puts her two young children on the school bus in the morning and to take time out to be there when they arrive home in the afternoon. Her job's autonomy and flexibility enables her to work from home or return to the office later in the day after her husband comes home from his job.

For eighteen years, Emily commuted fifty minutes each way to work, a requirement that greatly reduced her time with her family. Since this new job is only five minutes from her home, Emily has been able to enjoy the best of both worlds. Another pleasant surprise is that she has been able to eliminate the need for a nanny. Even though her current salary is less than she received at her old job, the savings has meant that her net income is close to what she was earning before.

It's been more than five years since Emily made the bold move to leave her secure job of many years. She now has achieved the balance she so desperately needed and has a job that challenges her intellectually and professionally and offers her autonomy and flexibility.

Emily created this near-perfect scenario by purposefully setting out to change her life, discovering what was most important to her, and then going out and finding a job that fit her Core Themes. Emily did it and you can do it, too!

PRINCIPLES FOR ACHIEVING HAPPINESS AND SUCCESS AT WORK
Consider the following: I believe there are only two goals in life—success and happiness. Success and happiness are personal and subjective. For some, success and happiness come from achieving a high position in their chosen field, earning large sums of money, or writing a novel. For someone else, success and happiness can come from the satisfaction of managing a nonprofit food bank for the neediest in the community.

What is defined as success and happiness is different for each of us. For example, the chef at a prestigious restaurant, who takes great pride in creating delicious and aesthetically pleasing meals, does so out of a personal sense of integrity and accomplishment. He achieves happiness behind the scenes from the accolades he receives from his boss and the restaurant's customers.

The owner of the restaurant, however, finds her success and happiness from engaging with the diners, in particular the regular customers who rave about the impeccable service and delicious cuisine. She has become a minor celebrity, who is well known to the notable diners who frequent her establishment. The many photographs and autographs of famous personalities, politicians, and successful business owners that grace the walls are testament to the success of her great restaurant.

Here we have two people, both in the same business but who define success and happiness differently. The chef is content to stay in the background, confident in his role and satisfied that his cooking is enjoyed by so many. He has no interest in being in the limelight. The owner is not interested in being in the kitchen preparing gourmet meals nightly. She prefers to play the role of hostess and interact with customers. If these two switched their roles, they would both be unhappy and not successful in their jobs.

Or take the third grade teacher who devotes her life to educating little "munchkins" with her primary goal being to prepare each child to enter the fourth grade. As the end of the year approaches, she no doubt works especially hard and spends the necessary time and resources to help those students who are struggling academically.

Success and happiness for this dedicated and responsible

teacher come from knowing she did her best to prepare her students to enter the following grade. When she returns in the fall, she has no expectations of receiving a "big, fat bonus" for her performance during the previous school year.

Now let's look at the teacher's best friend, who after college went to Wall Street and became a top performer in her investment management company. She also has worked hard and has dedicated her time and energies to achieving the highest level of respect from her superiors and her wealthy clients. Come bonus time, she expects and receives a large monetary reward for her excellent performance.

Success and happiness for this young wealth manager are derived from financial rewards and the respect and admiration of her peers, boss, and clients.

These two young, bright, and talented women chose careers that have brought them success and happiness. However, they have chosen very different paths. If these women switched jobs, both would be unhappy and likely unsuccessful as well. The school teacher is not motivated by money or the prestige of working in a large Wall Street firm, nor is the teacher's friend motivated by children's excitement at learning new skills or the modest paycheck that comes with the job.

Success and happiness are very personal and subjective. What makes one person happy may not work for another. Let me be clear: I do not judge the value of one career over another as long as each career is moral, ethical, and legal!

Most of us spend the better part of our life at a place we call "work." Since that is the case, it stands to reason we should explore what type of career will bring us the greatest satisfaction. What elements in your life are most important to you? Your health, certainly, both physical and emotional; your family and friends; your personal salvation, if you are religious, or your spirituality or belief system; and, of course, your career. While you may be well aware of what to do to improve your health, maintain your personal relationships, and tend to your religious life, do you know what is required to be happy and successful in your work?

KEY PRINCIPLES TO ACHIEVING HAPPINESS AND SUCCESS

Love or at least like (a lot) what you do for work.

Respect and get along with your coworkers and boss.

Believe in the company's mission, values, products/services.

These three principles can guide you to happiness and success in your career:

PRINCIPLE 1: LOVE WHAT YOU DO (OR AT THE VERY LEAST, LIKE IT A LOT)

Pursue a career in which you enjoy performing the basic functions of the job.

If you are a customer service agent, solving people's problems should be high on your list of enjoyable activities. If you're in sales, you should love talking to people and persuading them of the value of the product or service you are selling.

This sounds self-evident and maybe even simplistic, but many people ignore this basic rule at their own peril. These unfortunates harbor a deep dislike for the fundamentals of the jobs they do. I have counseled teachers who enjoy the subject they teach, but who dislike administrative and disciplinary duties. Physicians I have advised may love their patients but hate the bureaucracy of managed care or relish the intellectual rigor of medicine but don't like dealing with patients.

Early in my practice, I spent an enormous amount of

time on the road, presenting workshops to managers and leaders in cities across the country. While I loved teaching and interacting with these professionals, I detested the constant travel and the time spent away from my family. But those drawbacks were integral parts of my career at the time.

Eventually I concluded that the best part of those trips occurred when I pulled into my driveway. Recognizing what was most important to me, I cut out 80 percent of my travel, focused my business closer to home, and created a job that made me a much happier person. If I had not changed those aspects of the job I did not like, my unhappiness would have grown and had a negative impact on my life and work somewhere down the road.

Many mistakes and errors and poor performance on the job result when a person is stuck doing work he or she finds unrewarding and lacking in personal satisfaction. There could be many causes for this: the job isn't interesting enough; the job doesn't pay enough; the job isn't a match for the person's skills and abilities; the person is bored; the work is tedious and repetitious; the job is not what the employer described; the employee is burnt out after years of being in an unrewarding job; the requirements of the job causes a person to be anxious and stressed, affecting his or her personal life; the person had false expectations of what it was really like being a lawyer or a teacher or a nurse or a financial analyst.

Imagine the veteran teacher who once entered her classroom each day with boundless energy, excited at the prospect of stimulating her students' curiosity about history or English. Now, some twenty-five years later, she can hardly muster the energy to show up. What happened? Are her students getting the best value from her teaching? I think not.

What about the project manager who is fed up with

unrealistic deadlines and tired of dealing with unmotivated team members? Is he able to give his best performance under these conditions? I think not.

We all better hope that the auto technician who is rotating our tires loves what he does and is not disgruntled because the company reduced his salary or his benefits. Because if the technician is unhappy with his job and complaining to his buddy, he may not be paying close enough attention when he tightens the lugs. What about the actress who is performing the same role for the three hundredth time? How does she "get up" for playing her role night after night? At some point, she may begin to lose the energy and passion for the role. What about the theater goers who paid $150 for a fourth-row seat. Are they getting their money's worth? I think not.

Yes, we are all human and whatever we do is subject to human error. However, I believe that when competent people truly love what they do, they are more likely to perform consistently at a high level.

Once, as I dangled my legs from an examining table, the physician pointed to my left knee and asked how it was coming along. I said my left knee was doing great; it was my right knee that was the problem. Obviously, the good doctor had not reviewed my file before entering the room. Honest mistake and no harm done, but it did not inspire my confidence in him since he clearly was not up to date on the treatment of my knee.

The reality for many professionals is that at some point the job may no longer be satisfying. Therefore, it is essential that we constantly monitor ourselves to determine how we feel about our work. We have no control over changes in leadership or the hiring of a new boss or being assigned new responsibilities at work. However, we do have control over how we respond to these external changes that affect our feelings about our work. When you truly love and care about what you do for your life's work, everyone benefits.

PRINCIPLE 2: TEAM UP WITH COWORKERS WHOM YOU RESPECT AND WITH WHOM YOU CAN WORK WELL
You are likely to spend more time with your coworkers than with your family and friends, so your relationship with them is critically important to your happiness.

Do you go on vacation with people you can't stand? Or invite someone to dinner with whom you have nothing in common? Then why spend most of your time at work around people you don't like or can't get along with?

It can be difficult to control this element of workplace satisfaction. A few years ago, a professional colleague of mine stopped by for advice. He had a problem with a senior executive at his company, for whom he was quickly losing respect. The executive was dishonest, my friend told me, and did things that bordered on being unethical and even immoral.

My friend had begun to feel physically ill and emotionally stressed because of the situation, but he felt powerless to change his colleague's behavior. He had gone so far as to discuss the matter with the offending coworker several times, to no avail. Still, my friend stuck with the job.

A year later he came to see me again with the same complaint. He was unhappier than ever. Finally, he could take no more and, after weighing his options carefully, he resigned. Almost immediately he began to feel better. He had taken control of his life and had decided not to associate with someone for whom he had little respect. It took time to make that choice and courage to face the unknowns of leaving a good job for something else, but he simply had to do it; he could not accept his life the way it was. After his resignation, my friend began a new career free of the pressures he had faced. Today he is a member of a small technology consulting firm with colleagues he respects for their expertise and their commitment to running the business based on firmly held values which he shares.

I am not advocating leaving a job simply because of a few irritating coworkers in an otherwise good group of colleagues. We seldom find a group where everyone is a close friend. What will cause unhappiness is working in a group of people you do not fundamentally like or with whom you are not compatible. If you are quiet and respectful, for instance, you may have trouble with colleagues and supervisors who are loud, hard-partying, and disrespectful. Can you change their behavior? You can try, but you probably won't succeed. You will be better off changing your surroundings.

PRINCIPLE 3: BELIEVE IN YOUR COMPANY AND ITS MISSION
Make sure you like and respect what your company stands for and its products and services. Sharing your company's passion is even better.

How many of us can say that we truly respect our employers? Sadly, many can't, and that can be a big problem. If you don't care for or at least like your company's culture, you will find yourself on the outside looking in, and you'll never feel as if you're contributing to its mission. That makes you a lone wolf, not a team player, and it can lead to fundamental unhappiness. It can also transform you into a cynic, a career-killing behavior if ever there was one. Carrying cynicism to work with you every day hurts others, but it hurts you most of all.

When you work for a company you admire and share

in its mission, you feel comfortable in your surroundings and happy that you can contribute toward a larger goal, one that you believe in. One successful outdoor-apparel catalog company has developed a culture that its employees embrace. Almost everyone I meet from this company believes passionately in its mission and values. Employees have a uniform love for the company and consider it one of the best places to work in the country.

We live in an age of change. Companies merge and change strategies and leaders faster than ever before. As a result, corporate cultures are often in a state of flux. Among the biggest complaints I hear from longtime employees is that the company "isn't the same one I went to work for." Even when the change is for the better, it can alter the way you feel about the company.

One very important thing I have come to learn in my years of consulting is that a company's culture is a powerful force that influences how employees think and act. Many of my clients over the years have focused on their job's pay and benefits but failed to assess the culture of their employer. They eventually found themselves feeling out of sync with the company's cultural norms.

Every company and organization, like every family, has its own unique culture. Every city is uniquely distinct from every other city. The culture in New York City is different from San Francisco's culture. What is a good fit for one person may be totally wrong for another.

As you consider your career opportunities, it is very important to investigate the culture of the organization you may join. Make sure that its values, practices, and policies match your own. This will go a long way toward your finding success and happiness in your career.

How do you rate yourself on these three principles? If you like performing your daily functions and you enjoy your colleagues and your company, congratulations. But if, like many people, you come up short in one or more of these areas, you need to do some serious soul-searching.

If any one of these principles is out of sync, you are not likely to be fully satisfied on the job. Instead of enjoying your family or your hobbies, you will probably end up wasting your energy trying to cover up the fact that you don't respect the boss or that you don't believe in the company's products or services. Avoiding your coworkers becomes more and more difficult, especially in this era of cubicles and open offices. You can compromise and compensate for a while, but eventually your body or your mind will catch you in the lie.

Mark, a successful litigator, found himself in exactly that situation. He was in his thirties, a partner in a top law firm, earning a six-figure salary. But his enthusiasm for the law and its contentiousness was rapidly fading, and he found himself devising ways to avoid his responsibilities.

The demands of being a litigator no longer appealed to him; he especially disliked being constantly engaged in adversarial situations. So he hid in his office, spending more time reading the sports page than researching cases. That's a troubling sign in any field, but in the law, where careers rise and fall on the number of billable hours a lawyer submits to the firm, the avoidance of work is hard to disguise. When Mark came to see me, the senior partners had begun to catch on to his behavior. His anxiety about being discovered forced him to get help.

This talented young lawyer was astute enough to recognize the changes taking place within him—the rising worry, the moodiness, the feelings of uncertainty.

After much soul-searching, he was able to identify his Core Themes. He explored a career as an athletics coach at the university level. But after a cursory investigation of the academic credentials required to enter the profession, he and his wife decided that the timing wasn't right because of family responsibilities. Instead, Mark left the private law practice and joined the legal team for a large corporation. Here, he was able to use his legal expertise without the pressure of having to generate "billable hours" and the stress of being in court trying cases he hated. In his new role, Mark was much more content, had the stability of a regular job, and could now look forward to the future.

ROLE OF CORE THEMES

Core Themes: those unique, essential values, needs, and interests that define each of us personally and professionally.

Identifying Your Core Themes. Each person has on average seven to ten Core Themes. These act as a guide or road map to assist each of us in making intentional and deliberate decisions about the direction our career takes. Core Themes are unique to each person and must be followed if one is to find true success and happiness in one's life and career.

Let's examine Peter's primary Core Theme: Intellectual curiosity and learning. Peter is a highly intelligent financial professional who has a passion for learning and acquiring knowledge. Identifying his Core Theme has enabled him to focus on work activities that satisfy his intellectual curiosity. To stimulate his interest, Peter joined a team at his company whose role is to collaborate with information technology (IT) consultants to assure an efficient and cost-effective installation of new software. Peter also volunteered to serve as the financial support person for his company's new international division. He stays clear of the more mundane and practical aspects of his profession because they bore him. He has learned from the past that he loses interest in a job when he isn't challenged intellectually—a sure route to frustration and unhappiness.

Being true to one's Core Themes is analogous to honoring the vow of fidelity between a married couple. There is a greater likelihood that the marriage will be successful if both partners honor their vow (everything else being equal). However, when the vow is broken by one partner, a crack develops in the relationship that can jeopardize the marriage. Similarly, people who do not honor their Core Themes jeopardize their happiness and their success on the job. Core Themes are not optional if one is to achieve true happiness and success!

I believe that each of us has the potential to make important contributions to society. Knowing yourself at a deeper level is the first crucial step to identifying and understanding what that potential is.

Identifying your Core Themes provides the foundation and clarity to make clear, informed, and purposeful decisions about your life and your life's work. Discovering one's Core Themes requires four distinct phases. In the first phase, a person examines his or her personal and professional history to determine the knowledge and experience he or she has acquired. The second phase requires deeper self-discovery as the client pinpoints what is most important in his or her life and what he or she hopes to achieve. Phase 3 calls for the client to identify his or her own Core Themes. In the fourth phase, a person uses his or her Core Themes to develop a plan of action. In this proven method of gaining self-awareness, each phase builds on the previous one. With the passage of each phase, a person arrives at a deeper understanding of what is most important to him or her, ultimately identifying and using a unique set of Core Themes.

A person's Core Themes reside within his or her inner self. Unfortunately, many people's Core Themes lie buried beneath a pile of clutter or other obstacles that block a clear view of these most important elements. This book's goal is to help people uncover their Core Themes, an essential first step to greater happiness in life and in work.

In his book (with Bill Moyers) *The Power of Myth*, Joseph Campbell—author, professor, and mythologist— writes about finding one's bliss, which can only be found within oneself:

> If you follow your bliss, you put yourself on a kind of track that has been there all the while, waiting for you, and the life that you ought to be living is the one you are living. Wherever you are—if you are following your bliss, you are enjoying that refreshment, that life within you, all the time.

CORE THEMES BENEFITS

For those courageous enough to make the commitment to discover their Core Themes, life will never be quite the same. Taking the time to truly understand yourself, to see clearly what is most important to you in your life, can be transformational. Many of my Core Themes graduates report that they now view everything they do from the perspective of their Core Themes. They also say that they can more easily understand why other people are unhappy in their jobs, because they can see the clutter that keeps people stuck.

For some, it is like having a magnifying glass that crystallizes and sharpens the images. Core Themes bring complex issues into focus quickly and accurately. Consequently, you are able to make much better decisions concerning career opportunities and life in general.

One of my clients exclaimed, "I'd compare the Core Themes experience to visiting an ophthalmologist, whose goal is to help us see the world with a clear vision. Knowing my Core Themes has both broadened and focused my vision, so that the whole spectrum of my potential and my life's meaning has become visible, conscious, and clear to me."

Knowing your Core Themes and living by them enables you to be deliberate and purposeful in exploring career options and to arrive at the best decision. No longer are you confused or muddled about your choices. With Core Themes as a guide, you can take a logical, reasoned, and informed approach to your career decisions. How great is that?

Being clear about the direction you should take in your career makes a positive impact on all areas of your life:

- On a personal level, the stress and anxiety (both physical and emotional) experienced from months and years of feeling unhappy and unfulfilled are substantially lessened and often eliminated altogether. You suddenly have renewed energy to devote to your personal activities. Many report, "I have my life back."

- Family, friends, and yes, even the beloved pet benefit from your change in attitude and disposition as a result of having a career that is decidedly more rewarding. Everyone benefits when you return home at the end of your workday feeling energized and excited that you spent your day doing the things you truly love.

- Being in a career that is properly aligned with your Core Themes has a direct bearing on your productivity and performance. You are now able to take advantage of your true talents, skills, and knowledge to achieve the highest level of success on a continuous basis. Employers reap the benefits from having a more inspired and productive employee, and coworkers have a stronger team member. Everyone benefits!

- College students are able to be proactive and see clearly when choosing an academic major and relevant coursework. Recent graduates learn how to make the most of their education by being focused and purposeful. With such a heavy financial investment in earning a degree, doesn't it make sense to invest in learning what will really make you happy as you prepare to enter the real world?

There are broader benefits and rewards of living according to your Core Themes:

- You come to know yourself more deeply than ever before.
- You identify and rid yourself of the clutter that has kept you stuck in an unsatisfying career.
- You gain the courage and confidence to choose happiness over unhappiness.
- You have an action plan and strategy to explore and discover the career best aligned with your personal and professional goals.
- Most important, you have nailed down the unique Core Themes that will guide you for life. No longer will you be confused, misled, or unfocused. Clarity reigns and leads you to a more purpose-driven career.

Two

The Accidental Career:
How Did I Get Here?

*It is very common for people to "fall into" a career
with little objective thought, personal assessment,
or clear understanding as to what they want or
need. I call that the "Accidental Career."*

Many of us choose our careers with little objective thought. Sometimes we embark on them purely by accident. We seldom make a deliberate and purposeful choice about what suits us best or how we want to spend the remainder of our working lives.

Young people sometimes make decisions based on their preferences of the moment, not considering if the choices are right for a lifetime. An interest in sports leads to a degree in physical education. Love of fashion leads to a degree from a fashion institute, or a fascination with science to a biochemistry degree.

Most college students are nineteen years old when they declare their majors. How much do they really know about life and work? Do they have any idea how important such a choice may be?

One of my clients, Robert, was a CPA for a large insurance company. I asked him how he had chosen his profession twenty-four years earlier. He said his father had told him, "If I'm going to pay for your education, you're going to have to get a degree that will be practical and help you get a job right after graduation." Under those terms, he rejected liberal arts and chose accounting as a major.

"How do you like it?" I asked him.

"I hate it," he said.

"Then why do you stay in it?"

"That's an easy one to answer," he said. "Three children, a mortgage, and a golden retriever." (Big-time clutter.)

Robert's life outside of work pleased him. He loved his family and enjoyed volunteering in his community. Being involved with people brought him much joy, and his volunteer work became his real calling. But it wasn't enough to offset his lack of enthusiasm for accounting. He felt trapped by his obligations and his paycheck (more clutter).

Robert had what I call an "accidental career"—one he pursued without much thought about his real interests and goals. Accounting became a way to please his father and keep the college tuition money coming, so that's what he chose as a career. As it turned out, though, the job did not coincide with his Core Themes, the values, needs, and interests that were central to his life. When he finally understood the influences that shaped his career direction, he vowed to change course. This bright and talented man made one of the most important decisions of his life—to invest the time and energy to determine what would make him truly happy and successful. Not an easy task given the circumstances!

Robert had always had a fascination with the political arena, although he did not think it was practical (given his family obligations) to enter politics per se. After serious study, Robert chose to become a lobbyist for an organization he believed brought real value to people's lives.

THE CHANGING CAREER

You don't have to be who you think you are.
—Jeff Bridges (referring to Bad, the country singer
he played in the movie *Crazy Heart*)

Most of us change as we grow older and experience life. Our interests shift, our energies for a particular activity wane, and our attention transfers to other causes and pursuits. When we are young, we may be led in one direction, but by chance end up on a different road. Fate may provide us with surprising new opportunities that bring us joy, but only if we remain open to the possibilities and continue to reassess our needs and desires.

Serendipity—the vagaries of chance—led me to my career. As a young boy growing up in Massachusetts, I deeply loved the outdoors. I participated in a sport for every season, went hunting, and fished every chance I could. When it came to planning a career, I naturally looked for a job I could do in the wilderness.

Since I couldn't afford college, I worked in construction for a year after high school to earn money to study wildlife management. My dream was to work in Alaska as a wildlife biologist. In 1963 when I was twenty-one, I earned an associate degree from Nichols College. Shortly afterward, I enlisted in the army—a smart move for me, since enlisting allowed me to choose where I would serve, in the Alaskan wilderness.

I loved it in Alaska, although I wasn't as enthusiastic about military life. The army assigned me to Anchorage's Fort Richardson, which had a wildlife division on the base. Somehow I persuaded my superior officers to allow me to head up the base's wildlife operations, and for two years I conducted research projects on mountain sheep and moose. I even convinced my boss to hold the first-ever controlled moose hunt on the base. I spent my days in the mountains and wilds of Alaska and lived a wonderful and carefree existence, a dream come true.

During my time in Anchorage, I became involved in volunteer work for my church. In the process, I learned that I enjoyed helping people, especially youngsters. When my enlistment period neared an end, I asked my sergeant to submit my request for an extension that would allow me to stay in Alaska, where I could complete my bachelor's degree from the University of Alaska. Once I graduated, I planned to work for the Alaska Department of Fish and Game. Had that happened, my career would have been shaped by my early likes and aptitudes. But fate intervened, and I wound up following a completely different career path.

My sergeant forgot to put in my extension papers, and the army transferred me to Fort Riley, Kansas. Instead of working in the wilderness, I volunteered with a church in Kansas and began working with people again. I found it even more appealing than my work with wildlife. After my tour of duty ended, I left the military, went home to Massachusetts, met the woman I would eventually marry, and decided to study psychology, so that I could work in a field that allowed me to continue helping people.

As it turned out, I followed my interests to a worthwhile career. Those interests led me to discover what I really wanted, and that turned out to be something quite different from what I thought it would be. I traveled a journey of discovery, aided in my case by an absent-minded sergeant. Seeing my new opportunities required an open mind and a reevaluation of what I really wanted. Because I was willing and able to follow that twist in the road, I found a career that fulfilled my goals.

Some people, however, have a difficult time changing direction. Once they start down one road, they never bother to look around again. Even if fate intervenes, as it did in my case, they may not take the new path that presents itself. Most people don't regularly ask themselves if they are still satisfied or stop to wonder why they are doing what they're doing. But none of us is the same at forty-five as we were at twenty-five. Everyone changes, and you may need to change your career to accommodate the different person you have become.

In the movie *Crazy Heart*, Jeff Bridges played the role of "Bad," a washed-up country-music singer. In an interview about the movie, a reporter asked him, "What lessons can you take from Bad's life?" Bridges said that he loved the line in one of the film's songs, "I used to be somebody, now I'm somebody else." When Bad wrote that song, Bridges observed, he was probably thinking that he used to be famous, and now he was on the bottom of the heap. "But you can flip that coin around and say, 'I used to be an alcoholic, and now I'm looking up.' You don't have to be who you think you are." That's the great lesson Bad has learned.

CHANGES IN YOUR ATTITUDES/NEEDS/PERCEPTIONS

As a consultant, I traveled throughout the country giving workshops on various topics to business leaders representing a diverse group of industries. One of the more popular workshops was titled "Leadership and the Management of Change." The program focused on helping business leaders learn the basic principles of leading their organizations through the constant changes taking place in their industry as a result of the economy, restructuring of the organization, innovations in product lines, rapid growth, lack of growth, or other challenges.

In my introduction, I noted that change is a constant in life, business, and society as a whole. We cannot escape change unless we live our lives in remote seclusion. Therefore, we have to learn how to accept and adapt to the changes in life. This is not to suggest, however, that we have to like the changes.

As we progress in our life and our career, change is ever present. The young, idealistic lawyer who graduated from a top law school and is rewarded by landing a job in a prestigious firm soon learns that she needs to adapt to a political work environment where she has little to say. This is a very different set of circumstances from those she experienced in the law school classroom, where her ideas and thoughts were welcomed.

Now, years later, this same lawyer is struggling to understand and cope with the many changes in her law firm and the changing expectations of her partners and the community. Somehow, the practice of law changed from what it was when she first began her career some twenty-two years earlier. And, oh yes, she has changed as well! No longer is she as idealistic, open-minded, or optimistic. A bit disillusioned and more realistic, she, too, has learned to "play the game" in order to survive. The responsibilities of a growing family, increased pressures to produce at the office, and maintaining her expertise have taken their toll.

But, in spite of the changes, she continues to be successful. Success comes with a price, though, particularly when you have lost some if not all of your zest for the work. We will speak more about the negative effects associated with an unrewarding career in the pages to follow.

Change has a way of creeping up on us. Before we know it, we are in the fourth decade of our life and wondering why we are spending eight to ten hours a day working at a job we hate. And then there is the commute!

Since we cannot control many of the changes that occur in our life, whether they come from work, the government, or the environment, we must learn how to cope by adapting in the most effective ways possible. There is absolutely no good rationale for remaining in a career that has lost its value for you. To do so exposes you to physical and emotional harm that could seriously jeopardize your health and personal happiness.

EFFECTS OF HAVING THE WRONG JOB

Unhappiness at work can lead to a smorgasbord of symptoms that left untreated can cause serious health threats.

People who hate their jobs may develop stomach pain or nausea, frequent headaches, anxiety, depression, back pain, or other stress-related problems. Some clients have difficulty with sexual function; some drink more than they should. Sleep patterns change; stress prevents people from sleeping or causes them to sleep more than normal. I have had several clients who wore mouth guards to protect their teeth from the grinding brought on by stress. One client said that she had not slept through the night in more than two years. She often woke up in a cold sweat. Women in particular may use food as a means to cope with their unhappiness.

The mind may be able to hide the truth and dismiss the bad feelings, but the body cannot lie. It is a true barometer of one's real emotions. A wise person listens to what the body has to say.

Even feeling ill does not motivate some people to change their ways. They need added pressure to force them to get help, and usually someone at home provides it. Being unhappy in your job isn't usually confined to the eight or ten or twelve hours a day you spend in the office. It spills over into your home life, where it can hurt your spouse and children. This lesson was clearly illustrated at a workshop I conducted a few years ago for a group of managers from a manufacturing company on the West Coast. The subject was "Leadership and the Management of Change."

A senior manager, a stocky guy built like a defensive tackle, shared with the group a recent experience with his two little girls. He had been working long hours during the past few months and was frustrated that some of his projects weren't going well. He hadn't realized the stress he was feeling and how much it was affecting his loved ones until one evening when he came home from a long day at the plant.

As he removed his jacket, he could hear his daughters talking in the next room. He overheard one of the girls say, "I wonder if Daddy is angry again tonight."

At that moment, he told his coworkers, he understood how much the pressures from work had spilled over into his family life. Tears filled his eyes when he realized that his daughters actually feared him. Needless to say, the incident gave him the motivation he needed to reduce the stress at work. It also provided the motivation to get rid of the medication he had been taking regularly to cope with an unsettled stomach.

A spouse, a partner, or a close friend can be a terrific

gauge of one's career health, since a person seldom keeps unhappiness under lock and key for long at home. Loved ones serve as a sounding board for that unhappiness, sometimes listening for years to the same litany of complaints or worries. Eventually they grow weary of that role and may nudge (not always gently) the unhappy partner to seek help. A partner's feelings and reactions have a lot to do with how successfully someone can navigate into a more fulfilling career.

I always ask a new client how a spouse or a partner feels about the situation and what the loved one believes should be done. Interestingly, most clients tell me that their loved ones have urged them for months and sometimes years to make a change, advice they either ignored or resisted until they reached a crisis point. Many of my clients have denied the obvious for a long time. They have performed passably in an unsatisfying job, while enduring frequent moodiness or depression and ignoring the constant urging "to do something about it" from family and friends.

Why do these people continue to accept the pain rather than address the problem causing their unhappiness? What prevents even the brightest of us from seeing what is clear to so many people around us? For one thing, many people still subscribe to the old belief that work is work and that it doesn't matter whether we like what we do as long as we do it. That is an outdated belief and a sad one. Perhaps that philosophy had a place during the first half of the twentieth century, when many people had few options. At that time, workers had little control over their lives and few opportunities to improve their situation. They accepted their lot in life and were grateful for what they did have.

My father, a first-generation Italian-American, had to drop out of school in the sixth grade to help support his family. He compensated for his meager education by working hard at the only job he could find, strenuous manual labor at a local factory.

For thirty-eight years he worked as a machinist under horrible conditions. His job, which required him to run six or seven machines for up to ten hours a day, took its toll on him. Although he seldom complained, I knew he was not happy at work. When I was eleven, I visited my father's company and saw firsthand the sweatshop where he worked. The experience made a big impression on me and deepened my respect for him. I still remember that joyless factory, especially when a client tells me that he or she has little choice but to stay in an unsatisfying job.

My father and many of my clients have one thing in common. They learned to compensate for their unhappy lives on the job by immersing themselves in interesting and rewarding activities outside work. In my father's case, he became one of the most respected members of his community. For fifty years he devoted his time to the children of his adopted town, serving as a park commissioner and the president of the local Little League organization. Under his leadership, the park commission opened parks and built baseball fields that benefited the entire community. Finding ways to compensate can work wonders. Still the bulk of my father's day—and time—was spent doing a job he did not enjoy.

My father didn't have career choices, but you do. You do not have to remain in a job that doesn't meet your needs. Not only can you dream about something better, you can make your dream a reality.

The recession has resulted in millions of people being out of work—another reason that many remain in an unfulfilling job. After all, who in their right mind would voluntarily leave their job when the economy continues to be so dismal? Others remain stuck because they lack the confidence to embark on a career change. For many, it is a matter of evaluating the "trade-offs"—we love living in this community, the children are doing well in school, our relatives are close by and provide emotional support, there is no guarantee that the next job will be any better. The list goes on and on.

This is not to suggest that just because you are dissatisfied with your career that your only alternative is to leave. For many, this is the most extreme measure and resorted to only when attempts to change things have failed.

CLUTTER AND OTHER TRAPS

Clutter: a sort of mental noise, a messy chorus of thoughts that consists of rationalizations that keep us from making necessary changes.

The first step to achieving your dream is to get rid of the clutter that is holding you back. Too much clutter and you become stuck.

A misguided work ethic is one example of clutter. Many of us have adopted our parents' work ethic, a good thing unless it holds us in an unfulfilling job.

Marie, an accomplished clinical psychologist, held so tenaciously to her parents' work ethic that she couldn't get off the treadmill long enough to see what it was doing to her. She had worked long and hard for her Ph.D., an achievement that made her parents proud. But Marie wasn't happy. After fourteen years as a psychotherapist, she felt bored and trapped in her practice. Yet her work ethic kept her from acknowledging that she needed to try something else. The more she worked, the worse she felt. The worse she felt, the more she worked. It was a vicious cycle, and she was firmly stuck in it.

Marie solved her dilemma by slowly learning to carve out more time for herself. She gave herself permission to back off a bit and modify her work schedule so that it made sense for her. Eventually she realized that she couldn't stay in her current job because it was killing her spirit. She gave up private practice and went to work for a technology company. In her new job, Marie continued to use her skills and specialized knowledge, but in a setting that gave her more time and room to breathe.

For most of her life, Marie's work ethic served an important role in helping her achieve her goals. But that same work ethic, acquired from her loving family, became an obstacle that cluttered her thinking and blocked her ability to move on to a more satisfying career. Fortunately, Marie was able to free herself from the clutter and make better choices, which led to a more balanced life and a career that complemented her new lifestyle.

Clutter can be constant, annoying, and damaging. It consists of both real concerns and issues that are mostly irrational. Paying the bills, putting the kids through school, saving enough for retirement—these are real concerns that need to be addressed. Then there are the irrational concerns: what will your family think if you leave your job, what if you aren't smart enough to succeed at another career at your age, what will happen if you can't find decent-paying work again. These worries have the potential to keep you from making real and necessary changes. Do you really think, for example, that you—with a college degree, a record of accomplishment in your current profession, possessing drive and ambition—will never again find meaningful work?

Unfortunately, our brains do a poor job of filtering clutter. We don't sort our worries according to their quality or the likelihood of their coming true; they simply circulate in our heads, popping up at the most inopportune moments, disturbing our sleep, and keeping us from seeing our situation clearly.

Clutter consumes valuable energy. We become depleted, a natural consequence of wrestling with change and struggling with fear and confusion. My clients have myriad reasons for avoiding change:

- My daughter is entering an expensive, prestigious college, so I can't afford to leave my job now.
- We love where we live and don't want to move.
- I've been a retail manager all my life, and this is all I know.
- Security and stability are the most important goals in my life.
- I'm the "breadwinner" in my home, and we need the money my job brings.
- I've worked my whole life to achieve success and financial security. I can't give all this up just because I'm unhappy.
- We have a special needs child who is in a great program. We can't possibly consider a change at this time.
- My parents sacrificed to put me through law school. How can I disappoint them?
- The economy stinks; how could I possibly find a new job in this climate?

The list goes on.

What it really boils down to is this: "I'm afraid of change and the uncertainty of the unknown. Familiarity is comfortable, even if I'm unhappy."

Let's look at some of these rationalizations:

The children's education: Yes, it would be nice if you

could send your children to expensive private colleges. But at what cost emotionally, both to them and to you? Are you willing to sacrifice your own happiness for that goal? Would your kids want that? They probably would prefer to spend their childhood with a happy, relaxed, and healthy dad and mom. Besides, there are many excellent universities in the world, including state schools, with much more affordable tuition.

I don't know anything else: Sure you do. Inside you lies a wealth of interests, abilities, skills, and ideas that you haven't tapped. Now is the time to open your mind to the possibilities and explore them. One of the most exciting aspects of my work is helping people see the range of talents and skills they already possess. The typical American is better educated, better trained, and better prepared to enter the world of work than ever before. New and exciting careers beckon that didn't exist ten years ago. For most people, fear and a lack of confidence are the real barriers to finding a different career. Choose to be proactive and assertive instead of passive.

The relocation issue: This is an understandable obstacle to change. You love where you live. The kids are settled and doing well in school. The family enjoys great friends and a wonderful community. Under most circumstances, this would be difficult to give up. But if you're not happy with your job, sooner or later you may have to consider moving. Something has to give.

I can't give up my security: There is no security! The days of a lifetime job are long gone. Today you have to make your own security. Your job—the one you have stuck with for so long through happy and unhappy times—could literally disappear overnight, leaving you with a severance check (if you're lucky) and bad feelings. True security rests in only one place, and that's in yourself.

I can't admit I failed: This is another common rationalization that has no place in your search for a satisfying job. Ask yourself why you continue to do work that's unrewarding. Why does leaving or changing a career have to be considered a failure? Reflect on where this belief came from in your life, and then consider the benefits you'll derive from having a job that makes you happy. You will become a better parent, a better spouse, and a better person when you use your talents in a fulfilling career that reflects your values, needs, and interests—your Core Themes.

This does not mean you should make big changes lightly or without careful preparation. The opposite is true. It is critical that you think long and hard about your life before you take any calculated risks. You need to have a clear vision of your options and the compromises involved in changing your situation. Still, the bottom line is that there is no excuse for wasting the rest of your precious life being unfulfilled and unhappy.

Not long ago I read a newspaper story about a wonderful, adventurous couple named Brad and Barbara Washburn. Brad Washburn was a respected cartographer and mountaineer when he met and married Barbara sixty-one years ago. Together, they climbed mountains all over the world and mapped Mount McKinley, the Grand Canyon, and Mount Everest, all while raising three children and writing books about their adventures.

The reporter asked the Washburns for the secret to their long marriage. "We've taken a lot of calculated risks together," Brad told him. "If you go all the way through life without risks, you'll have a hell of a dull life."

Amen.

I came across a survey that was done with people eighty

years of age and older. One of the key questions asked in the survey was: "As you reflect back on your life, what would you do differently." When I ask my clients what they think these people said, I commonly get, "Well, they probably would have spent more time with family, or they wouldn't have worked so hard, or they would have traveled more, etc." All reasonable responses. However, the overwhelming response from these elderly men and women was: "If I could do one thing over in my life, I would have taken more risks."

When you are eighty-two, will you be thinking with regret about your decision at age forty-two to pass on the opportunity to buy that fly-fishing outfitting business in Bozeman, Montana? Or when you, at age fifty-five, for security purposes, decided to stay in the same job with the same company rather than accepting a position with a "start-up" organization that would have been more exciting and growth-oriented? Or when you turned down the opportunity to take a position in a foreign country because your spouse convinced you that stability was more important than a serious career change? Or about the idea you had for a new product that you had been working on but never had the courage to borrow against your home equity to get the business off the ground? The list goes on and on.

Yes, when you are looking in the rearview mirror, it is easy to think about what you would or should have done many years earlier. But, unfortunately, not many of us have a crystal ball that allows us to see into the future and make all the right decisions. That's where the risk comes into play. You have to make these decisions at a moment in time when you may not have all the information you would like and when you have no guarantee that your idea or opportunity will be successful.

There are a host of reasons why most people work for companies and businesses. One key reason is that there is minimal risk. The owners, investors, and founders have taken the risks. But when you don't take calculated risks, you, like many of the elderly respondents in the study, may feel disappointed later in life when you look back and wonder, "What could have been?" "If only I..."

In general, most people tend to play it safe in life and stick to what is familiar and comfortable.

Whenever you feel trapped and can't quite imagine which way to turn, think about that observation. Sometimes you have to take risks. Without them, there can be no big payoffs.

My client Lance, a former human resources professional turned artist, has this quote displayed on the wall of his studio:

Life is not a journey to the grave with the intention of arriving safely in a pretty and well preserved body, but rather to skid in broadside, thoroughly used up, totally worn out, and loudly proclaiming, WOW! What a Ride.

—Author unknown

If you are unhappy, give yourself permission to change. It's a good first step.

THREE

Deciding to Get Unstuck

My clients are a diverse group. They include students, teachers, lawyers, doctors, recent graduates, stay-at-home moms/dads, accountants, nurses, members of the clergy, and professionals from the business world. Some work in the private sector and some in nonprofit organizations; some haven't worked in years, and others have just graduated from college. They are different in many respects, but most have at least one thing in common: they are seeking careers that are satisfying and meaningful and in which they can make a difference.

Some come to me on their own because they can see no future for themselves in their current field, while others are referred by their organizations because it has become clear they need career counseling of some sort, either because of their performance or because they have asked for assistance. Some are referred by their companies for outplacement—that is, they are leaving their employer, voluntarily or otherwise, and are being offered my help in finding a new job or career.

Many of these people see themselves as powerless actors reading from a script they cannot change. They have many concerns: The boss is a jerk who doesn't appreciate what they do; the company is no longer what it used to be; the work has turned into drudgery, thanks to new government regulations or new technology or changing practices in the industry.

It can take time for some people to accept the notion that they themselves are fully responsible for their lives. When they do accept that concept, a dramatic and positive change takes place. They realize that they have the power to control their life's direction and take the wheel again. At that point, an explosion goes off inside their heads. Almost always they realize what they need to do.

As I listen to them, I can begin to understand their feelings and thoughts, clues to the struggle they're going through. Eventually I steer the work we're doing to a deeper truth—that with few exceptions, they are all living the lives they chose, happy or not. Some are simply unhappy by choice.

Before you object to that statement, think about it for a moment. As much as we are unhappy about our circumstances, we have, in the vast majority of cases, chosen to remain where we are. Sure, it is difficult to walk away from a lucrative corporate vice presidency because you disagree with the firm's values, but you can do it if you so choose.

You can experience just as much joy earning your living as you do cheering for your daughter's soccer team or fly-fishing for trout in Montana—well, almost. You don't have to stay in an unrewarding job. You can choose instead to be fulfilled. Choice. Indeed, it is the message that I've stressed over and over to my clients during the twenty-eight years I've coached and counseled people on their careers.

THE CHOICE IS YOURS

You always have options. You don't have to remain in an unsatisfying job or work for a bad boss. To travel another road, however, you must search your heart for the answer to this question: What do I want to do with my life? Finding the answer often requires help. Even the brightest of us are capable of great self-delusion, especially during times of unhappiness and stress, and we often need to learn a new way of evaluating ourselves and our potential. I wrote this book to help people who are at a point in their lives when they need guidance in defining who they are and what they want. Whether you are entering the workplace for the first time or after many years at unrewarding jobs, this book will provide important tools to help you make the best decision possible.

I'm not suggesting that the options are easy or that it's always as simple as just walking away from your work. We all know that's usually unrealistic. All of us have felt familiarity's dull comfort or the reluctance to leave a profession we've worked so hard to master but no longer enjoy.

Once we begin exploring options, however, we gradually become open to the possibilities of change. It always amazes me just how much a responsible person can do to improve an unhappy situation when his or her mind opens to those possibilities.

Turn your considerable talent toward finding work that satisfies you. Granted, you'll have to make compromises, giving up some of the things you value in return for others that you value more. The key, of course, is seeing more clearly exactly what it is that you value.

No one forced you at gunpoint to become a sales manager instead of an engineer or a chemist instead of a poet. Somehow you made a series of choices that led you to where you now find yourself. Perhaps you were influenced by a teacher or by the glamour of the job or by the lure of being rich. More likely you simply took the route that seemed the most practical, given your interests at the time.

Just as you made these choices originally, you can now choose to change direction. Remember that you are in charge of your life—you and no one else. You can choose to remain unhappy and unfulfilled, or you can choose to have a satisfying life simply by taking a different path.

By placing the blame for your predicament on other people or events, you give away control of your life and allow them to steer your course. Real change takes place when you accept responsibility for your life and its circumstances and make a commitment to change. That commitment can come only when you look at your life dispassionately and objectively and search inside yourself for explanations about how you got where you are.

If you choose to continue working for someone whose values you can barely tolerate, that choice is yours. If you're still working in the family business long after it has become clear that the fit isn't right, that's your responsibility.

You are where you are by choice. The sooner you accept that fact, the closer you will be to finding a new path.

That's reasonable, right? So why do so many well-educated and accomplished people fail to see it? The answer is, in part, because of the clutter in their minds. Luckily, there is a cure for clutter. It begins with making a personal commitment to change and the will and discipline to face up to your clutter and sweep it away.

I first thought about writing this book almost twenty years ago. It seemed to me then that far too many people led unhappy professional lives. With my practice growing and my time short, I put off the project. Now, in the twenty-first century, I believe this book is more timely and important than ever. The economy has both expanded and contracted, and mergers and reorganizations have driven home the lesson that job security is an oxymoron. Time seems shorter, the demands on us greater. The world has been shaken by horrifying acts that remind us of our mortality and make us want to lead better lives. More people than ever are searching for real meaning and purpose.

For me, personally, real meaning and purpose come from helping people find greater happiness in their lives and their work. It's not always easy, but finding the path that's right for you can be the most rewarding and satisfying journey you will ever take.

ANYBODY CAN BE A CORE THEMES CANDIDATE

My clients show me every day just how unhappy some people can be in their chosen careers. My sunny waterfront office in beautiful Portland, Maine, is the setting for story after story of frustration, sadness, anger, uncertainty, worry, and illness. These stories aren't told by malcontents and underachievers but by smart, accomplished people who don't understand how things could have gotten so bad and who don't have a clue where to turn next.

I work with people from all kinds of businesses who bring with them a variety of complaints and problems. Some suffer from depression and benefit from medical treatment for the disorder. For most, depression is a symptom of something else: a lifetime of wrong choices or of choices not made at all. Something isn't right in their work, and it is making them miserable.

Expending energy on activities you hate, especially over

long periods of time, wears you down and affects other aspects of your job and your personal affairs. No job is perfect, and each of us has some aspect of our work that is unpleasant or even objectionable. Most people understand and accept this as a reality. As long as the time spent doing disagreeable tasks is kept to a minimum, we can usually get by without serious damage to our bodies and our emotions. Sometimes, however, that isn't possible. Consider Todd's story:

When Todd walked into my office a few years ago, it was clear he was in trouble. Todd had started his career as a teacher in the town where he was raised. He was terrific at it. He loved kids and education—teaching seemed to be a perfect career choice for him. As is often the case, Todd's abilities made him a natural candidate for promotion.

When I first saw him, Todd was forty-five years old and a high level administrator of the school system where he had begun his career two decades earlier. Success had come at a huge cost. Todd's weight had skyrocketed to 250 pounds, and he was tired and anxious—by his own admission, a physical mess.

Todd told me, "I love my day job, but I hate my night job." He meant he still loved education, the students, and the teachers, but the administrative and political parts of the job were killing him. He especially dreaded the biweekly school board meetings (his "night job"), where board members, parents, and teachers regularly skewered him.

I spent six hours with Todd during that first meeting. Before he left to return home, I said, "I hope we have enough time to help you. You're a cardiac arrest waiting to happen." He laughed nervously, but I told him I was deadly serious.

Fortunately, Todd spent the next weeks working hard to gain the self-knowledge he needed to turn his life around.

After our first meeting, Todd and I explored every aspect of his career: his likes and dislikes, his belief system, his needs.

After several weeks, Todd put together a list of what mattered most to him—his Core Themes. His family, his health, and his love of kids and education made the list. A fat paycheck and the prestige of a big job didn't. The exercise made Todd reassess his job, and he decided to resign. But he had to address one stumbling block (clutter) before he could do that. His father still lived in the town where Todd worked, and he clearly enjoyed his son's success. Todd worried about what his father would think if he left his prestigious position.

Eventually Todd got up the courage to tell his father about his decision. Not surprisingly (to everyone but Todd), his dad immediately gave his blessing to Todd's plan. What Todd had worried about—that he would lose his father's approval, a big issue at any age and a prime example of clutter—had in fact never been a problem. His father only wanted him to be happy and saw his son as a success no matter what he did for a living.

Todd was still wrestling with two questions: "Do I still want to be a school administrator?" and "Do I want to stay in the education field?"

Todd decided to accept a position in a smaller community where he felt he could make a real difference (and where he would have to deal with only one school board). Two years later he made another big decision: to leave his position entirely and accept an appointment as human resources director for another school district. The new job allowed him to use his expertise in education while avoiding the onerous duties he experienced as an administrator. His prayers were now answered!

Todd is where he belongs, and he's a much happier

man. He paid attention to his Core Themes and, in doing so, learned what was really important to him. He had the courage to act and to set a course toward a more satisfying life.

Todd found himself in a job for which he was not well suited. In fact, his work hurt him physically and emotionally. Yet he felt powerless to change his situation, and the inability to make things better for himself only compounded his misery.

It's a common problem.

Many of us make career choices for what seem like good reasons. We like a subject in college or excel in it and that leads us to choose it as a major. Sometimes a good opportunity comes along at just the right time. Perhaps a campus interview results in a job offer and that opportunity becomes a career. We may choose to work in a certain field because we want the money or the prestige it offers, or because others in the family have pursued the same career.

For a while, life is satisfying and good. We are young and open to experiences. We learn our new jobs and develop the skills to perform them well. Raises come, and so do promotions. We become authorities, then experts. Meanwhile, we get busy with other parts of our lives. We fall in love, marry, have children, and buy ever-bigger houses and expensive automobiles.

Time speeds by. We're in our late thirties, forties, or fifties, still working in the field we chose fifteen or twenty or thirty years earlier. But something is wrong; something is missing. The enjoyment we found as a twenty-five-year-old isn't there anymore. It's been replaced by boredom, frustration, and emptiness—maybe even anger. We're miserable, and somebody must be to blame. Yet we believe there's little we can do about it. We become lulled by our lives, always short on the energy required to think about change. We have golden handcuffs: a regular paycheck—often a big one—and other people who depend on us.

The trap has been sprung. We're stuck.

We may not consciously know what the problem is. All we know is that something isn't right. We may have trouble sleeping, or sleep too much. We may be irritable for no apparent reason. Or we may not be able to concentrate.

I once had a client, a lawyer, who grew to hate trying cases so much that he sat in his parked car before work, trying to talk himself into just one more day on the job. Another client displayed his unhappiness by hiding in his office; voicemails and e-mails went unanswered. Interestingly, neither man was sure exactly why he was so unhappy. These were not slackers. They were extremely successful people, overachievers, who had simply reached a state of internal chaos.

A Different Work Environment

There are many reasons we find ourselves in that condition. Some have to do with the evolution of work in the modern world. Professions expand or contract, requirements change, expectations grow or diminish. Ask the physician who rankles at the restrictions managed care imposes on her practice. Or the teacher who finds the children of today more challenging and their parents less supportive than in the early years of his career. Or the attorney who complains that he's being forced to spend too much time developing new clients and not enough time practicing law. Or the businesswoman who can barely keep up with the many demands on her time because of layoffs her company was forced to make due to the recession.

Technology has dramatically changed the way business

is conducted in the twenty-first century. With new and ever-changing technological advances, we are expected to respond faster and faster to the demands of our colleagues' and customers' requests. No longer can we say, "I'll be out of town for a few days and not available." We send e-mails and text at all hours of the night and early morning and expect an immediate response. Many of us have allowed technology to control us instead of using technology as a tool. These changes in the American workplace affect the way we spend our workdays.

There are even deeper reasons for the epidemic of career dissatisfaction around us. One is that the baby boom generation—that huge population of Americans who started life in the years just after World War II—is reaching the age when people typically begin to question meaning and purpose in their lives, sometimes with great urgency. Time is growing shorter, and they wonder: Was I born to be an accountant all my life, manipulating numbers day after day, year after year? Am I doing anything with my life that adds value to society and the community?

I believe that within most of us lies a deep need to do something meaningful—something that gives satisfaction to our soul and provides a spiritual reason for being.

This is especially true for those of us who have worked hard to achieve something in our lives. Sometimes that need simply isn't fulfilled by our work. Often we find fulfillment instead from the non-work parts of our lives. We glory in the accomplishments of our children, for instance; we watch them in school plays and on athletic fields, and we live vicariously through them as they negotiate college, find love, and start their own families.

Our loved ones can and often do provide joy. If we're

lucky and we work hard at it, our husband, wife, or partner is our mate in every sense of the word and plays a big role in making us feel whole.

Avocations, too, can give us a sense of well-being. Our hobbies and volunteer activities—whether it's football, fishing, or serving on the school board—can teach us valuable lessons, show us how to laugh and enjoy ourselves, and lead us into becoming more involved with the broader world. A beloved pastime allows us to feel alive, if only for a weekend or a week's vacation each year.

For many people, though, that isn't enough. In reality, hobbies and outside activities are often a means of compensating for what is missing in our work. To be truly fulfilled, we need to find satisfaction in every part of our lives, and that means that we need to find fulfillment in our work.

Life is not perfect, and neither is work. Jobs that we might otherwise find satisfying are filled with frustrations; sometimes dream careers have to be performed in less than satisfactory surroundings.

The premise of this book is not that we can find perfection, but that we can be happier and more productive if we are courageous enough to use our knowledge about ourselves to make the right choices.

Life is about pragmatism and about making our work and our existence the best they can be.

So your career isn't the best it can be. You've made compromises, maybe some that have left you unhappy with yourself. Why should you rock the boat at this point in your life? Change, after all, is hard.

The answer is obvious: because you're wasting a huge amount of your life if you're not happy at work. Most people graduate from college in their early twenties and work well into their sixties. During those forty-plus years, a typical worker will be on the job from forty to sixty hours a week—that's eight to twelve hours daily, the majority of your time awake. Do the math. Think about how many hours you devote to your career. In fact, we spend far more time with our coworkers than we do with our loved ones and close friends, and often with far less happy results.

Imagine spending even a tenth of that time, a very long time indeed, doing something you hate. Add it up over the course of your life, and think about the monumental waste of your time. Do you really want to throw away that irretrievable time?

Many of us have already spent an hour or more engaged in the work of the day before we even get to the office. If you're like me, you start thinking about what's ahead as soon as you jump out of bed and realize that it's Monday, not Sunday. You think about work while you shower, eat breakfast, navigate the expressway, and park the car. Then, at the end of the workday, you decompress and think about how the day went. Work is never far from our thoughts.

If you're satisfied with your career, you're expending energy in a positive way. If you aren't satisfied, if your job bores you or requires you to do things you don't want to do, the energy you spend thinking and worrying is wasted, and you feel drained. Too many people live their lives that way.

Life Is Not a Rehearsal

David Brudnoy, Ph.D., who for many years hosted an evening radio talk show program on WBZ in Boston, made the most of his shortened lifespan and the time he spent at work. Dr. Brudnoy, who also lectured at Boston University, was an intelligent, provocative, and stimulating talk show host. He always had interesting topics and was always well informed and knowledgeable about the issues discussed, as were his guests. You didn't call in to offer an opinion unless you were ready to be challenged by Dr. Brudnoy or his guests.

One evening he dropped a bombshell on his listeners. He revealed that he was gay and was returning to his home in Minnesota to discuss his situation with his father before he heard the news from other sources.

In the next few years, after being diagnosed with HIV (and later full-blown AIDS), Dr. Brudnoy hosted his radio program sporadically as illness took its toll. Then, for about a year and a half, he was in remission, and his voice and energy returned. Listeners could hear the renewed vigor when he was on the air. Dr. Brudnoy's bout with cancer and near-death experience after being in a coma for nine days brought about an even stronger desire to experience life—and his broadcasting work—to the fullest.

Dr. Brudnoy used the time he had left to write *Life Is Not A Rehearsal*, a memoir in which he describes candidly and honestly his life as a gay man who espoused libertarian conservative views and beliefs. The book helped educate people about AIDS and homosexuality. The day before his death, in December 2004, Dr. Brudnoy made his last radio broadcast from his hospital bed.

Unfulfilled Workers, Lost Productivity

Unproductive hours at work are not just a waste of your time; such behavior affects everyone around you. When you accept a job, you have struck a contract with your employer. In return for money, office space, administrative support, a computer, health insurance, a vacation, and sick days, you have agreed to provide a certain service. Job dissatisfaction decreases the value of that service to the company, your co-workers, and your customers. It affects the way you view yourself and the way you interact with others, including your loved ones.

I have been conducting an informal survey of my clients for several years now. I ask them how productive they are on any given day. In other words, how much of the workday is spent doing the company's work and how much is frittered away at the water cooler, surfing the Internet, making personal calls, or sending e-mails and texting to friends instead of preparing for meetings and getting projects done in a timely fashion.

On average, my clients report that they spend 70 percent of the workday on company business. That means 30 percent is spent on something other than work. That adds up to one and one-half days each week, six to seven days each month, and about seventy-five days each year. That's a lot of unproductive time. Would my clients be willing, I ask them, to write a check to the company giving back 30 percent of their pay? The smirks on their faces say, "Are you kidding?"

If you are not committed to your job, you are not fulfilling your end of the contract. That is neither fair nor responsible behavior. It hurts productivity, lowers morale (including yours), and infects others. Are people happy working at only 70 percent of their capability? I'll bet they are not. In my experience, most mature professionals want to be productive and do a good job. They want to accomplish something, not feel as if they are treading water or throwing time out the window. They don't like feeling as if they're breaking the contract. They have pride and a strong work ethic, and it just doesn't feel right when they're not fully engaged. Yet the work wears them down and dulls their efforts.

There are other costs associated with this lack of fulfillment. When we are unhappy at work, our families can pay a
heavy price. We become tense, moody, and less able to enjoy
our lives. Sometimes we complain so much that our loved
ones feel almost as helpless and frustrated as we do.

So how can you become unstuck? What can you do to
be happy at work? If you've been nodding your head as you
read this, if the scenarios of unhappy workers sound familiar, then you have taken the first step toward finding a more
fulfilling job—and a more satisfying life. Acknowledging that
you have a problem is the beginning of the journey. The second step is deciding that you want to change things.

CORE THEMES BASICS

Once you decide to make changes in your life, the Core Themes
program guides you through four phases toward your goal.
The first two phases are perhaps the most important because
they hold the key to success for the other phases. Both focus
on you, who you are, and what you want out of life.

During Phase 1, you will focus on your personal and
professional history (knowledge/experience) and all the stages
of your life, from childhood to the present. You will also
undergo a series of tests and surveys to assess the following
areas: primary interests, intellectual abilities, personality profile (temperament, traits, characteristics), key skills, communication style, motivational profile, emotional intelligence,
and other attributes. Those seeking to apply the Core Themes
program on their own (without the help of tests) can gather
much of this information by honest self-examination.

Phase 2 takes you to a deeper level of self-discovery.
You will explore what is really important in your life, what
you want to accomplish, and why. Your written responses to

these questions will help you identify your Core Themes later on in the process. These exercises call for you to reflect on what you value most. They require you to examine seriously your life and the way you live it.

In Phase 3 you will use the knowledge you have gained in phases 1 and 2 to identify your own Core Themes. You will consult family members at this stage to help you develop your unique road map to happiness and success. These strongly held values, needs, and interests will guide you toward a fulfilling life at work and at home.

Phase 4 focuses on developing a plan of action, using your Core Themes to point the way. You will network with mentors and conduct interviews with business leaders in fields that interest you, always keeping your Core Themes in mind. These strategies will lead you to decisions and choices in your life and your career that are best for you.

You can lead a happy, productive life—if you make meaningful changes based on what is important to you. The following chapters will tell you how to make those changes so that you are living your passion, guided by your own personal, unique Core Themes.

FOUR

Phase 1: Getting to Know You

The first step to gaining career happiness and success is a crystal clear understanding of yourself.

The Core Themes program is a powerfully probing process during which you learn what is most important to you in order to achieve true success and happiness in your personal life and in your career. Truly knowing yourself at the deepest level possible is key to identifying and understanding your unique Core Themes. Yet it has been my experience that too many people simply never take time to examine seriously who they really are, how they got to be the person they have become, and why they do what they do.

The central premise of my Core Themes work is simple—if I can help you understand yourself, if you can truly know yourself, then you will make better decisions in all aspects of your life. You will be more intentional and purposeful in all areas of your life, and this will have a direct effect on the lives of those who mean the most to you. When you live your life in a more intentional manner, you will make decisions based on your strongly held beliefs and principles. Your choices will make sense to you as a result.

Take Larry, for example. When Larry came to see me, he knew he was unhappy, but he had no idea why. The symptoms were clear enough: anxiety, a feeling of desperation, problems sleeping. Beyond that, he had no idea what was troubling him. Larry had worked at a successful retail company for the past twenty-two years and had been a top executive for a decade. Despite his success, he did not enjoy his job. "I go to work and feel empty most of the time," he said. "There are days when I feel like a fraud, that I'll be found out."

One of several children, Larry came from a home where money was always short. He overcame that poverty through plain, old hard work. "My wife and I can't believe the money we make," he told me. "I never dreamed that I could have achieved so much."

He and his wife had three children and a grandchild. They lived modestly and had everything they wanted. So why, he asked, am I so unhappy? He'd been miserable for a few years. A spiritual person, he felt an absence of meaning and purpose in his work and in his personal life, as well. That weighed heavily on him.

Larry was like many of the people I see in my practice. He had a bad case of the clutter and too many internal distractions to get an accurate idea of where he was and where he wanted to be. He was out of touch with himself. He needed to sort out what really mattered to him. Without that knowledge, he was leading a life that only occasionally satisfied his needs.

At my suggestion, Larry spent several sessions with a

therapist, who helped him learn how to manage his anxiety and stress. Once he had done this, he worked on identifying the values and goals that were important to him—his Core Themes. Larry came to the realization that his life was out of balance. He had devoted most of his time to developing a successful career that earned him stature and recognition among his peers and provided his family with financial security. In the process, he had lost touch with the most important people in his life, his wife and his children and most important, himself.

As he progressed through the Core Themes process, Larry began to shed much of the clutter that had kept him trapped in a career that had long since lost real value to him. As he began to think about and identify what was most important to him, he realized that he needed to carve out a life that was more balanced. This meant that he had to adjust his intense work schedule to make time to repair a damaged marital relationship, to become more involved with his children's lives, to renew his Christian faith, and to devote time to his personal and psychological well-being.

Once he sorted through and identified his Core Themes, Larry regained control of his life. He made serious adjustments to his work schedule. This commitment to achieving balance in his life made it possible to improve the quality of his marriage and attain other personal goals.

On the professional level, Larry discovered that he wanted a career that gave him a sense of personal fulfillment, required a variety of skills, and provided a fast-paced work environment. Having greater clarity and perspective on what was really important in his career, he became involved in strategic projects, which gave him a renewed sense of passion and excitement that he hadn't felt in several years.

WHO AM I?

Knowing ourselves at a deeper level is what enables us to make the right decisions for our lives. Sometimes it takes sessions with a therapist to reach an understanding of oneself and identify life experiences, events, and special people who have shaped our values and beliefs. For others, deep reflection can bring the required self-knowledge.

It is surprising how little time we spend thinking about who we are and who and what we want to be. We go to the dentist every six months for a checkup. Once a year or so we go to the family doctor for a physical. Most of us get our car inspected every year, and even the furnace gets a once-over every fall. Yet we spend few moments, if any, thinking deeply about our attitudes toward our work, which occupies a good portion of our lives. Even when we recognize that we are not happy in our job, we often do nothing about it. We wait as months and years tick by, passively accepting our fate.

That's too bad. Don't wait until it is too late to ask yourself if you are truly happy in your work. Are you doing what you really love? Do you derive enough satisfaction from it? Are you still deeply interested in your profession? At the end of your life, will you be pleased with how you have spent your time and what you have accomplished?

Many people don't ask those questions. They go to work every day, do their best at their jobs, return home, enjoy their families, and get up the next day and do it all over again. Only when they reach a crisis of some sort do they begin to think seriously about changing their routine.

There is a more rational and enlightened way to live, and it involves learning about yourself—how you became the person you are, what led you to choose your career, what satisfies you about it, and what doesn't. Self-discovery is a

crucial part of formulating your Core Themes. You didn't get to be the person you are today by accident. Whether you realize it or not, you made many choices along the way that have shaped you and led you to the life you now live.

If you are to be happy, what you do for your life's work has to be related to what you believe is most important. For you, work isn't just the means to an end—a way to pay bills, save for a vacation, or send the kids to day care. The work itself must have value, meaning, and purpose.

To get started, here's an exercise. Answer this elemental, but hardly elementary, question: "Who am I?" Write down as much as you can about yourself. Describe in detail your personal traits, talents, and beliefs. What responsibilities do you have? What roles do you play in your life? How do you define yourself? By your job title? By what you do? By your possessions? By your activities? Are you a spiritual or religious person?

Ask yourself this, too: "How would my closest friends and family describe who I am?" Would their descriptions match your own? Would your coworkers' descriptions resemble yours? In order for the self-discovery process to work, you must be totally honest and willing to explore, with no barriers or off-limit areas. And you must accept whatever emerges from your study of yourself.

This journey of self-discovery led one of my clients to admit reluctantly that he was often negative about many things in his life. He didn't like being that way and didn't fully understand why he was negative. During his study of himself, he realized that he overanalyzed his thoughts, which made him indecisive and led him to procrastinate. These insights inspired him to examine his relationships, his interactions with his staff, and the causes for his unhappiness in recent years. The self-knowledge he gained from these investigations gave him the answers he had been seeking—and a guide to creating a fulfilling life for himself.

Knowing yourself at a deeper level and recognizing the need to change make it possible for you to develop a plan that allows you to do what you want to do in your life and your career. For my clients, self-discovery is a two-step process. The first step involves a thorough examination of their life history. We begin at childhood and discuss every phase of life to the present. They describe their lives, their work, their problems, their hopes, and their values. We focus particularly on special people and events that had a major impact on their lives. During the second step of the process, an objective assessment, which includes tests, surveys, and questionnaires, reveals clients' abilities, interests, personal profile, communication style, and motivations.

As you reflect on your own life, think about the people, events, and situations that influenced your development, thoughts, beliefs, values, behavior, and decisions. Review your life history, including your family dynamics, physical surroundings, emotional atmosphere, and childhood dreams.

Next comes the assessment phase. The comprehensive assessment consists of twelve standardized tests, questionnaires, and surveys designed to reveal a person's internal motivations, personal and professional values, interests, abilities and aptitudes, skills, knowledge, emotional intelligence, and personality. These tests should be conducted by a professional who has the skills and experience to interpret the results correctly.

Readers who do not wish to undergo the complete battery of tests still can go through the assessment process on a more informal level. Instead of relying on formal tests, you can unearth portions of the same information by interviewing yourself, asking fundamental questions about your life, and assessing what kind of person you are. You will need to dig deep and commit yourself to completing the investigation, but the results will be well worth the effort. At the end of your study, you will know yourself at a deeper level, which will give you a clearer sense of the direction you want to take in your career. I spend a lot of time guiding people through this process. This book will teach you to do the same kind of exploration on your own. So let's begin to discover the real you.

THE FORMATIVE YEARS

To understand ourselves, we need to go back to the beginning. We operate according to values and beliefs we learned as children, but sometimes we aren't aware of how these lessons influence our current behaviors and decisions.

We each have our own unique history. One person may come from an abusive home, another from a loving family. Some were young when their parents divorced, others lived in foster homes or with a large, extended family. *You didn't get to be the way you are by accident.* Whatever your life experiences, they have in some way shaped your values, beliefs, behaviors, and often, your career choice.

In the case of Marie, the clinical psychologist mentioned in Chapter 2, the work ethic that ran her ragged and kept her from enjoying life was ingrained in her from her earliest days. It was so deeply embedded in her personality that she never really thought about the ways in which it controlled her life.

When I asked her where she had learned to work so hard, she seemed puzzled by my question. As we discussed her life as a little girl growing up in her family, however, she realized that she had learned her work habits from her hardworking parents and had accepted them as part of her value system.

She began to understand that, just as she had learned such work habits, she could unlearn them or modify them as she chose. That insight enabled her to begin making changes in her work schedule. She realized that she could modify her behavior without rejecting the loved ones who had instilled the habits in her. Marie started making time for herself. She took piano lessons, something she had wanted to do for years but had never found the time to do. She allotted time each morning to walk along the beach with her dog. She was now taking charge of her life, and it felt positive and productive.

By uncovering clues from your history, you, too, can make meaningful changes in your life. Let's begin the self-interviewing process. Set aside some quiet time—no phone, television, or kids—in a favorite place where thinking comes easily. It may be helpful to take notes or write down your thoughts in an essay or a memoir. Tell the story of yourself.

THE EARLY YEARS

Begin by asking yourself questions about your childhood. Be honest. These are not idle questions; take them seriously and think hard about your responses:

- Describe where and when you were born.
- Describe your family structure (parents, siblings, pets).
- Describe your father—type of work, level of education, personality, behavior, interests, involvement in family matters and relationship with the children, relationship with his wife/your mother. Your father's current age, health. If deceased, when did he die and how? Your father's background and anything that you think is unique about his own history.

- Describe your mother (same as for father).
- Describe your siblings—personality, role in family, your relationship with each, current status (married, children, profession). Is your relationship different now from the one you had when you were children?
- Looking back, what was your family like? What memories do you have, positive and negative. Do you have clear or vague memories of your childhood? Why?
- How would you compare your family to other families you were familiar with when you were a child? What did it feel like as a member of your family? Do you have warm feelings or negative feelings about your family?
- What was the single most important influence your mother and father had on the family?
- Reflecting on your childhood, do you think of your family experience as a healthy one? If not, why?
- Describe yourself as a young girl/boy growing up as a member of your family (active, quiet, athletic, studious, mischievous). What type of student were you? How did you differ from your siblings and friends?
- If I had the opportunity to interview your mother and father, how would they have described you as a child?
- How did your father/mother's work influence your family and you in particular?
- Did your parents remain married? Were both parents alive and well during your childhood?
- What was your family's socioeconomic status?
- Reflecting on these early years, what is the experience or memory that most comes to mind?
- Other thoughts and memories?

Early influences can play a crucial role in setting one's life course. Charles was the chief financial officer of a successful corporation. During our interview, he told me that his father had owned a small manufacturing company and had come to hate the business in later years. Discussions around the family dinner table typically focused on the business, and usually the news was not good. His father complained about the economy, the lack of orders, and the pressure he felt to make the weekly payroll and cover other expenses.

Charles heard his father say many times how he wished he hadn't continued with the business, which his own father had started many years before. Seeing that unhappiness, Charles vowed that he would never become part of the family business, and he didn't—he chose another path altogether. Thinking about that early motivation helped him to realize more fully why he had made the choices he had. Such early influences shape your life whether you know it or not.

THE HIGH SCHOOL YEARS

- Describe yourself as a student, courses you enjoyed, activities both in school and outside. What classes/activities did you excel in? How would your best friends describe you?
- Describe your favorite teacher. Why did you like him/her? What influence did teacher(s) have on you, if any?
- As you matured into your mid- to late-teens, what changes occurred that set you apart from your younger self?
- What is the single most important experience or memory you have from your high school years?
- Are you still friendly with any high school classmates?
- Did you date? If so, describe your experiences.

As a teenager

- Were you moody or even-tempered?
- Did friends seek you out for advice?
- Were you shy? Outgoing? Confident?
- Did you have misgivings about your looks or body?
- Were you an outstanding athlete, one of the smart kids, or popular because of your personality? Or did you feel like you were outside the mainstream, socially speaking?
- Did you think of yourself as average? As someone who fit in with everybody? Or who didn't fit in at all?

Sandra was extremely reserved and quiet as a young girl. She also wanted to succeed, and she wasn't about to let her shyness keep her back. She pushed herself to get involved with group projects and volunteered to do presentations. Her efforts paid off: she became a successful bank executive. Sandra's lesson is one that may apply to you. She knew her weak points and worked hard to overcome them. Although we are all born with certain traits, we don't have to let troublesome ones get in the way of reaching our goals. We can choose to learn new and different behaviors.

Milestone experiences—those events that have a major impact on us—can influence the course of our future lives. Think about moments in your own life that affected the way you think or act:

- Is there an event that changed the course of your life?
- Did someone's words or actions cause you to change your view of yourself or spur you to do (or not do) something?
- Can you identify turning points in your life? What drove you to take one path and not the other?

Mary, whose family was poor and who grew up on the wrong side of the tracks, remembers well her encounter with a guidance counselor during her senior year in high school. Mary had just received the results of her scholastic aptitude tests (SATs), which turned out to be better than she had expected. She rushed to share them with the guidance counselor. Instead of celebrating Mary's success, the guidance counselor told her that she wasn't college material and that she should think about getting a job instead of applying to schools.

Mary left the office despondent and in tears. Other people's opinions have the power to change our lives—if we let them. Mary resisted that particular quagmire, however. Rather than allowing the experience to beat her down, she became more determined than ever to make something of her life. She got into a good college and now has a successful career as the vice president of advertising for an established technology company. To this day, Mary's memory of that encounter with her guidance counselor is a primary motivation for her, and it accounts for much of her success.

A person's view of himself also has a great deal of power over his life and what he does with it. Think about how you saw yourself as a teenager:

- How did you feel about your sexuality as you were growing up?
- Did you like yourself?
- How would you describe your self-esteem as a young person?
- Why did you feel that way?
- Has your view of yourself changed since childhood?
- What impact did your view of yourself as a teenager have on your life?

Turn the clock back to when you were seventeen or eighteen, on the brink of starting a whole new life experience—college, work, travel, military:

- Reflecting on the years up to that point, what are the experiences that come to mind?
- Did you move into the next chapter of your life with hope and eagerness to experience what lay ahead or with fear and apprehension?
- What important lessons did you learn during this time?

When I think about my own experiences, I vividly recall how much I wanted to attend college. My family could not afford to send me, and I hadn't saved enough money to pay the tuition. So, while the rest of my friends headed off to school, I took a job with the New England Power Company and for the next year dug holes to submerge power line poles in inaccessible areas. My best assignment was as the assistant to the bulldozer operator. I learned a lot from this experience, including the value of hard work and the discipline of saving for college. I was exposed to older men in the construction business who taught me much more about life than I knew. I began taking the first steps toward controlling my life by making choices that led to greater independence.

What themes and threads run through the chapters of your life? As you delve into your past, ask yourself how those early experiences, lessons, and memories affect you now.

The young-adult years

Now it's time to examine the next phase of life: the young-adult years, the period from late teens to mid-twenties. During this time many young adults go to college, some marry, some enter the military, and some go straight to a career or job. Whatever the circumstances, this is a crucial time during which we lay the groundwork for our futures.

When you think about it, it is truly amazing that we often make some of the most important decisions of our lives when we are so young. How little we knew about life and work then compared to what we know now! Consider some of those major decisions:

- If you chose to attend college, how did you go about selecting a major?
- How did you end up at Ohio State or Middlebury or UCLA?
- Why did you choose a small liberal arts school instead of a big state school, or vice versa?
- Did you fall in love with the campus? Or did you consider it the best school of the choices available to you?
- Why did you make the choices you did during that period of your life, and what did your decisions say about you?
- What made the single biggest impact on who you are today?
- Do you feel as if you squandered your time, or did you use it wisely?
- Did college have an impact on you? Why or why not?
- What was on your mind during this time?
- Why did you decide to join the family business?
- So, you left Boise to seek fame and fortune in the big city. What were you thinking at this time in your young life?
- Did you make your life and career in the safety of your small town because leaving seemed scary?

William was in his early twenties when he sought me out because he was unsure about his next steps. He had beaten cancer as a teenager, which delayed his graduation from high school and gave him a late start in college. An intelligent and sensitive young man, he earned a degree in English and now was faced with his future.

He had chosen his major because he loved to write, especially poetry. Studying the great writers, he said, had taught him much about life. Now he wanted to have an impact on the world through his own writing.

It was a crucial time for this young man. What should he do? Continue his education in graduate school? Give up his dream, temporarily at least, and become a newspaper journalist or enter the business world? Or should he take a job that paid him just enough to live on so that he could devote most of his time to his real passion, writing? Will he look back when he's forty-three and be happy with the decision he made at twenty-three? Or will he, like so many others I've met, look back sadly at the dream he gave up?

As is often the case when people are at a crossroads in their lives, William floundered for quite some time before he settled on a career direction. He had made the initial decision to study English and the great writers without really considering any of the practical consequences. For so many of us, life has a way of influencing our decisions. For William, the responsibility associated with a serious relationship, the sense that time was speeding by, the intense desire to settle on a direction (not just any career direction but a career track that was practical and stable)—these all led him to explore the field of information technology. To his surprise, he discovered that his writing talents, analytical ability, and intellectual curiosity fit perfectly with his newfound career. William hasn't given up writing poetry, but he views his passion for writing as an avocation and his career in the field of technology as his true vocation.

William's story is a familiar one. Fortunately for him, he was persistent in his efforts to bring focus and clarity to his life and career. His experience also offers an excellent example of how one's Core Themes can be realized in a variety of professions—sometimes in a career one never had before considered. Core Themes are constant and don't change easily, but the manifestation of one's Core Themes (how one lives them) can vary depending on various factors.

What were your early twenties like? Take a few minutes to revisit those days. Tell your whole story, and don't rush through it. If you are currently in this stage of life, what is it like for you? Are you pleased with the decisions you have made so far? Do you feel you know what career path you wish to follow? Or, like William, are you struggling in your effort to sort out the pros and cons of the next chapter in your life?

THE TWENTIES-PLUS YEARS

Whether you attend college or not, at some point you wake up one day to find that it's time to enter the real world. You have to be truly independent; it is sink or swim. You can get a job, join the military, go to graduate school, or backpack across Europe.

Whatever your choice, you probably have no idea where it will lead. Maybe you get a teaching degree or work for IBM. Little do you realize that that decision may determine what you'll be doing fifteen or twenty years later. Most young people begin their careers without a clear plan for their life. It's a critical time, yet we seldom reflect on the consequences of our choices. We're being launched, but where will we land?

After graduating from a well-known New England college with a degree in English, Matthew found himself in the middle of a recession. He struggled unsuccessfully to find a job, then headed west to Wyoming when life didn't turn out as he had planned. Nine years later, he makes a living as a fly-fishing guide and freelance writer. He's also working on his first novel. In Matthew's case, fate and circumstances played a critical role in his life and career by presenting him with an unexpected choice. It worked out well for him; he's married, he owns a home, and he's happy.

Not everyone is as lucky as Matthew, who saw an opportunity and followed it, with his values and goals firmly in mind. Many people, however, allow an unexpected turn to disrupt their life plans. They drift along without knowing where life is taking them. Instead of thinking about what they want out of life, they let life happen until one day they discover they are terribly unhappy and they don't know why.

Many recent graduates, eager to be on their own, move to big cities. Those without high-paying jobs soon learn that fending for themselves is a daunting task. Freedom is not free after all—the city can be cold and expensive. For some, their first professional jobs after college provide excitement and fulfillment. But others undergo a big letdown with their career choices. It's easy to become disillusioned and not know which direction to take. Often, inexperienced young professionals resort to trial and error in an attempt to stabilize their lives and careers. Without a plan or a sense of purpose, however, this usually leads to disappointment.

It may take several years to figure things out. For many, this can be a time to experiment by working for different companies or running their own business. A person's final choice of career may be influenced by luck or by advice from friends, family, and colleagues.

This period is crucial, since the decisions that are made can affect a person's life for many years. It's important to think about what direction you want to go and why. Think about the plans you made as a young adult and how you responded to unforeseen twists of fate:

- What were your plans as a twenty-something? Did you even have a plan?
- What was the job market like?
- What pressures did you encounter?
- How did you deal with your life at the time?
- What did you learn about yourself?

My experience with many of my twenty-something clients is that they are often disillusioned. After spending a great deal of time earning their academic credentials at a high financial cost to them and their families, they often find themselves in a state of confusion. The hopes and dreams they had as they studied and worked their way through college have been dampened by the poor economic climate they faced when they graduated. Frustrated at failed attempts to find meaningful employment, they flounder and become even more discouraged. How did they get to this point in life? What happened to the promise that a good college education would provide financial security and career happiness?

THE SETTLING-IN YEARS

Before you know it, you've reached the "settling-in" years. Life suddenly becomes more complex than before. You've become a grown-up—married with a family and a mortgage, or single and traveling the world, with little time to develop close ties or a personal relationship. A few years later you find yourself with more experience in your chosen field and more responsibilities, as well. Long gone are the carefree twenties.

These days many young adults wait longer to settle down in relationships. Many focus on their careers and put off serious dating and marriage until their thirties. The career a person chooses at this stage of life can play an important role in his or her personal life. Alternatively, the choices a person makes in his or her personal life carry over to the workplace.

Sandy had worked for a catalog company for twelve years, loved her job, and was successful at it. Ambitious and bright, she always had focused her energies on climbing the corporate ladder. She took every opportunity to advance and moved several times to accept promotions.

Suddenly her life changed. She met the man of her dreams, and overnight her priorities shifted. Soon she was engaged to be married. Like others reaching this stage of their lives, Sandy found it necessary to reassess her goals and make some course corrections. She still enjoyed her work, but she was no longer willing to travel extensively or relocate for the company. Sandy's solution involved finding challenging and interesting projects in the home office that satisfied her intellectual needs but didn't require her to travel as much.

Life is filled with trade-offs. In Sandy's case, her need for love and happiness took precedence over an all-consuming ambition at work. Knowing your Core Themes and using them as a guide will enable you to make informed, purposeful, and deliberate decisions that will bring fulfillment as your life and your needs change.

So, you are settled in your career. Consider the answers to these questions:

- How is the job treating you?
- Are you satisfied in your choice of career?
- Has your work life turned out as you thought it would?
- Given where you started, do you like where you are?
- Have you made career choices that you wish you could make over again?
- Do you still like teaching, project management, practicing law, managing a retail store, or are you continuing to do your job because it is what you have done for fifteen years or because it provides financial security for your family or because you fear the unknown (clutter)?

Julie asked herself those questions. A thirty-six-year-old attorney, she was on track to become a partner, a dream job for some but not for Julie. She wanted a more fulfilling career that would allow her to serve humanity.

After examining her life and identifying her Core Themes, she became a United Way executive. The new position allowed her to use her many skills, perform satisfying work—and earn a third of her previous salary. It was a good move for her, and she accomplished it by honestly answering her own questions.

Perhaps you aren't quite burned out yet. Maybe you've just started to question your career choices. In any case, take the time to ask yourself why you are in your current job and whether you are there for the right reasons.

THE MID-LIFE CHAPTER

Congratulations, you have made it through the settling-in years. Now you are a seasoned pro with twenty-five years of job and adult life experience behind you. Your kids are in college or on their own. You are in a mature relationship. You look at life with aplomb and more than a little humor, and you know that you won't have another fifty years on this earth.

This may be the first time that you've ever really taken stock of your life. I have clients who have spent thirty years in their chosen fields only to conclude that they just aren't happy anymore. They have joined the ranks of those who seek more meaning in their everyday lives. If you feel your life needs some readjustment, consider the answers to these questions:

- What do you think of your life so far?
- Do you want to continue with what you're doing, or do you feel a change would be good?
- How do you feel about getting up and going to work in the morning?
- Now that you've risen in your business or attained senior status, does your career still excite you?
- If you own a chain of hamburger restaurants, do you still care passionately about how the hamburgers taste?
- If you're a senior retailing executive, do you still get excited walking onto the sales floor?
- Does teaching Philosophy 101 to sophomores still make your life worthwhile?
- Do you ever ask yourself, "Is that all there is?"

At this stage of your life, your career isn't the only thing that's maturing. You are, too. It's time to realize that life is beautiful and still full of options, if you choose to exercise them. The worst place to be is stuck and unhappy.

Seasoned workers have a tremendous amount to offer

the world, but sometimes they need to figure out how their rich experience can be used in areas that are unfamiliar to them. Soon these mature workers will be considering winding down or retiring, raising an important question for them: What will they do in the next chapter of their lives?

I'm fascinated by the fact that many of my clients separate their skills into work and non-work categories. Often they discover they can reap rewards when they bring skills from one arena to the other. Bret, for example, was a forty-three-year-old computer programmer, whose boss praised him for being highly competent in technology-related areas. Organized and precise, he accumulated an extensive knowledge of various computer programs.

When he was young, Bret had wanted to be a professional musician. Outside work, he spent his spare time making music. Bret played percussion in a band made up of several guys his age and wrote much of the music the band played. He found little opportunity, however, to express his creative talents at work.

Unfulfilled at work, Bret decided to go through a developmental assessment. The assessment consisted of a review of Bret's personal and professional history and a battery of career tests and surveys. The data collected from the assessment showed that Bret was both right- and left-brain oriented. In other words, his aptitudes included both analytical thinking and creative problem solving. After a series of discussions with his boss and a human resources professional, Bret took on higher-level technology projects and became a key contributor to the company's new information technology architecture plan. The expanded creative opportunities provided the fulfillment that had been missing in Bret's job before he put his Core Themes to work.

Examining how the past has shaped us gives us the power to assert control over ourselves, our decisions, and our actions. As children, we cannot choose what we are exposed to—our family's religious faith, the food served us, the home we live in, or the nature of our family life. As adults, we can elect to change the behaviors that resulted from our upbringing, provided we are aware of them.

Think about your own personality. If you were a sensitive, moody child, chances are that you continue to show that side of your personality from time to time, and it probably has affected your personal relationships, your attitude at work, and how you view the world around you. While that sensitivity will probably always be part of your character, you don't have to be controlled by it. You can control it.

As you review your personal history, you may awaken old feelings from the past. Understanding those feelings and discovering what evoked them often can lead to substantive change. Once we acknowledge our feelings, we take an important step toward being accountable, a key attribute in a mature and responsible adult. Delving into family history and upbringing can also bring out the reasons behind a person's reluctance to leave an unfulfilling job.

Susan, a successful but severely overworked brokerage executive, is a perfect example of how self-examination can lead to real change. Susan had given so much of herself to her high-pressure job that she had forfeited her personal life. She worked well into the night and on weekends. The phone rang incessantly. She constantly had to deal with more problems than she could possibly solve. In return for performing this difficult job, Susan had an impressive title, a high salary, and power.

Why had she pushed herself so relentlessly when it was

clear that she was burning herself out? Early on in our work together, she had no answer to that question. But as time passed, clues began to emerge from her childhood. Susan was the "ugly duckling" of her family, the child no one expected to succeed. Her mother frequently reminded Susan of her shortcomings. Yet despite the self-esteem problems this caused, Susan had enough intelligence and inner steel to prove everyone wrong.

She became the most successful of the family's children by far, but at a huge cost to her well-being. As she examined her roots, she realized that her low self-esteem from childhood was contributing to her self-destruction as an adult. That discovery alone was enough to steer her away from her manic work schedule and onto a career path with a much saner pace that she could control.

Is your work a good fit for the person you are? As alluring as they may be, a high salary and prestige may not be the answer to your prayers. After conducting his self-analysis, one of my CEO clients decided that he was not cut out to be the top dog. He didn't like the constant politics of his job and dreaded dealing with Wall Street analysts. His real love was technology and how he could put it to use creatively to make a difference in the organization. Like many competent, driven professionals, he got caught up in the heady importance of his job and the advantages it brought and allowed himself to stray from his Core Themes. Now that he has refocused on what is important to him, he is back on track and doing work that fulfills him.

It may seem odd that we could live for forty or fifty years without really understanding why we believe certain things, or without even knowing that we do. That is why self-discovery is so important. It can help answer the crucial question "Who am I?" and another one of equal importance: "What can I be?" Only by asking yourself these kinds of thought-provoking questions and answering them as honestly as possible can you begin to judge what you need to do to find fulfillment.

It may be helpful to step back and reflect on the thoughts and feelings this self-review has evoked:

- Now that you've thought about your life as a whole, what observations did you make?
- What conclusions did you reach?
- What did you learn about yourself?
- Are you better able to put some things in perspective?
- Most important, when you think about your unique history, what are the things that matter most to you?
- Do you have a better grasp of how you developed your values and principles?

Your answers to these and other questions will form the basis for the self-discovery that is essential as you forge your own unique Core Themes.

FIVE

Assessing Your Strengths and Weaknesses

Knowing Others is Wisdom.
Knowing Yourself
Is Enlightenment.

—Lao Tzu, old master
and father of Taoism

The second major piece to the discovery process involves assessing your strengths and limitations. This knowledge will help determine your suitability for particular types of work. By probing these topics, you are in a sense becoming better acquainted with yourself. The results of this self-study will help you understand why you got into your line of work in the first place, why you perform as you do, what keeps you where you are, and what kinds of jobs suit you best.

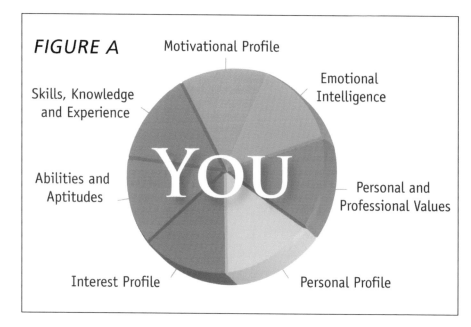

FIGURE A

Motivational Profile

Emotional Intelligence

Skills, Knowledge and Experience

YOU

Personal and Professional Values

Abilities and Aptitudes

Interest Profile

Personal Profile

SKILLS, KNOWLEDGE, AND EXPERIENCE

We all gain knowledge as we move through life. Some of it comes from education, but much of it develops as a result of life experiences—from role models, travel, athletics, work, play, reading, music, and many other aspects of life.

Think about the knowledge you've acquired and the skills associated with that knowledge. Consider professional knowledge but also all of the other areas in which you consider yourself knowledgeable. You may have been an English teacher for fifteen years, but now you yearn to do something different. At this stage in your life, though, you think that the only job you know how to do is teach Shakespeare to sixteen-year-olds.

Consider the skills you have acquired as a teacher. Here's a short list:

- You know how to develop plans.

- You are comfortable making presentations in front of people.
- You write well.
- You are a good listener.
- You have learned to help people solve their problems.
- You are organized and disciplined.
- You are personable.
- You are articulate.
- You are skillful at running meetings.
- You know how to keep people interested and inspire them.

In fact, many educators have skills that are essential in private-sector jobs. They do especially well in human resources, and they make excellent trainers and facilitators.

As an exercise, make a list of the skills and knowledge you've acquired in your own life and career. In addition to listing a particular skill—your knowledge of financial accounting standards, let's say—take note of the broader attributes required to learn that skill. Among other things, learning accounting standards takes patience, a grasp for the intangible, and the ability to study, all of which are skills that can be transferred to other jobs.

As you construct your list, bear in mind that sometimes your knowledge may be different from your skills. For example, you may have the knowledge of how to build a house, meaning that as general contractor, you hire the architect, oversee the subcontractors (framers, electricians, plumbers, sheetrockers, and others), order the lumber and other materials, and so forth. However, you do not have the skill required to wire the house or sheetrock the walls.

Think hard about your various life and work experiences. Include travel, study abroad, research work, projects, and seminars and workshops you have attended. Perhaps you played in a band while in college or high school, or you represented your school on the debate team, or you may have spent time in the Peace Corps.

Some of you may have grown up in a military family, living in several countries before reaching your teen years. Or your mother may have been a politician, and you witnessed her campaigns and met prominent people at a young age. Or perhaps your father was an accomplished minister, and you grew up in a "bubble" with little privacy.

What learning experiences enriched your life during your college years? Did a year abroad change your perspective on life? These and other personal experiences all have contributed to shaping the person you have become. Some of the items on your list of skills, knowledge, and experiences will be redundant. That's a good thing, because it suggests an important factor to consider as you attempt to clarify your career direction.

Step back and review your list. What is it saying about the person you have become? Are you actively using the knowledge and experiences you have accumulated throughout your life? Think about the skills you have acquired. Do you still enjoy using those skills? If so, are you taking full advantage of your skills in your current career?

ABILITIES AND APTITUDES

Success comes from doing what we do best and using our full abilities and talents. To do this, however, we must be able to recognize what our true abilities are and find the niche where they can best be realized.

Discovering your abilities and aptitudes is a key element

in the Core Themes program. Consider how you think and how you go about solving problems:

- Do you have an analytical approach toward your job?
- In other words, do you spend a lot of time questioning why and how something works?
- Are you adept at scrutinizing and sorting out the essential elements of a problem?

The answers to these questions will help determine what kind of job is best for you. Highly analytical people, for example, may be less fulfilled in a setting where there is little opportunity for rigorous investigation, while people who rank high in conceptual skills, those who understand complicated facts and see the "big picture" quickly, are likely to grow bored in jobs where there is little opportunity for intellectual stimulation. I've heard many managers who have a high aptitude for strategic matters express dissatisfaction with jobs that center on tactics—in others words, not where to go but how to get there.

Your intellectual abilities and interests also help determine the type of job that will satisfy you. Think about how your intellect meshes with the work you do:

- Do you need to be intellectually challenged in your work?
- Do you hate repetitive tasks and get bored once the execution of your ideas is under way?

If you answered yes to these questions, you probably rank high in analytical and conceptual skills. If solving problems isn't part of what you do at work, you may feel intense boredom with your job.

As you might expect, most intelligent people know they

are bright. When you were in school, you may have compared well to others in your class. Teachers, parents, and friends commented on how "smart" you were. Your test scores confirmed this impression. Surprisingly, though, you may not be using your full intellectual abilities on the job. Many sharp young professionals with little experience find themselves assigned to monotonous, tedious, and unchallenging tasks.

Consider one young woman who recently graduated from a prestigious law school. As a student, she was fully immersed in academia, learning the theoretical underpinnings of law and being intellectually engaged in research and stimulating class discussions.

The law firm she joined after graduation gave her assignments that were essentially grunt work. She spent most of her time digging for information in the library to assist the senior partners, who prepared the cases. As you might expect, she grew frustrated at having to pay her dues in this fashion. She wanted to be where the action was. For the young lawyer, that problem usually is solved over time, as he or she works up the ladder toward partner—that is, if the novice can last that long. Senior managers and their companies might have better luck retaining bright young employees if they found creative ways to take advantage of their talents. Seasoned professionals, too, often benefit from taking on new challenges, which can in turn aid the firm.

Perhaps you have been blessed (or cursed) with the gift of gab. When you speak, people listen and are impressed with your ability to convey complex information in simple terms. This ability has been a key factor in your success; therefore, it is critical that you continue to engage in work that allows you to present your ideas to your colleagues. Being confined to a cubicle doing technical work would frustrate you. Even though you could express your views electronically, you would miss the personal contact and the energy that comes from immediate feedback from others.

It is important that your abilities and aptitudes play a prominent role in your day-to-day work. This will put you one step closer to achieving real satisfaction in your career.

EMOTIONAL INTELLIGENCE

There is more to success than academic achievement. In recent years there has been much research and discussion in the workplace about emotional and social intelligence. Thanks to researchers like Daniel Goleman, the author of *Emotional Intelligence* (1995); Reuven Bar-On and James D. A. Parker, authors of *The Handbook of Emotional Intelligence* (2000); and Cary Cherniss, who with Goleman authored *The Emotionally Intelligent Workplace* (2001), we have a broader understanding of intelligence. We all learn differently and apply our knowledge in different ways to achieve a certain level of competence.

Those who rank high in emotional intelligence have a greater ability to understand emotions, both their own and those of others, and this ability allows them to make the most of their other skills. Emotional intelligence contributes to self-awareness and helps us to manage our feelings. At the workplace, emotional intelligence helps us understand other people's needs and motivations.

Gail, a successful property manager for a large real estate company, grew up in an upper-middle-class family. She was exposed to the best schools and cultural advantages. But Gail recognized early in her life that traditional academic study was difficult for her. She performed adequately but fell far short of what was expected of her academically.

Gail managed to get through college and earned a degree. In time she developed a reputation as someone who always got the job done. She became a tough negotiator who fought to get the best leases for her company. She even taught a course on negotiating at a respected university. Because she wasn't "polished" and didn't come across as erudite, however, her company failed to promote her. In fact, Gail had a high degree of emotional intelligence, a quality that enhanced her ability to deal with other people and served her well in her job. When a new boss joined the firm, he recognized her talents, and she won a promotion and the recognition she deserved. Making the most of her "street smarts" and practical knowledge, Gail became a successful and respected professional.

Gail's story shows that you don't have to have a high IQ or graduate from a prestigious university to achieve success. In her case, a high EQ (emotional intelligence quotient) brought her a successful career.

Are you skilled at interpersonal dynamics? At a meeting, do you instinctively notice other people's behavior (change in tone of voice, facial expressions, ways they express themselves)? Or do you often miss these verbal and nonverbal cues? Have you been puzzled by your inability to influence your boss or coworkers to support you on a project?

Emotional Intelligence can be learned, but it takes time, practice, a good coach and, of course, the motivation to learn. In my practice, we use various instruments to measure EQ. The MSCEIT (Mayer-Salovey-Caruso Emotional Intelligence Test) has been one reliable way to measure a person's emotional intelligence.

Some people have an innate ability to "read" interpersonal cues. Psychologists, successful sales people, human resource professionals, management consultants, teachers, nurses, and those in similar fields tend to have high emotional intelligence. The primary focus of their work is helping people. Consequently, they spend a great deal of time on developing their emotional intelligence so they can relate to their clients or customers.

In general, professionals coming from the hard sciences such as information technology, computer programming, engineering, laboratory science, and accounting tend to have less well-developed emotional intelligence. It may be that they simply have limited contact with people and consequently have little opportunity to develop this ability.

PERSONAL PROFILE

Next, let's examine your temperament, traits, and characteristics—those elements that define you and make you unique. Your personality is a blend of many traits and attributes. We'll touch on only a few to give you a sense of how important your personal style and temperament are to your life and career.

Some of us are high-energy people, and we tackle our work with gusto and a sense of urgency. We move quickly and sometimes frenetically—the typical "Type A" personalities. Others are "pacers," more content to take their time. Pacers measure their actions and have a more deliberate style. Your approach toward an activity also depends on whether you like or dislike the task, the expectations of others, and your own assessment of how the task should be accomplished.

The high-energy person is typically best suited to work in a fast-paced business, preferably with coworkers who approach tasks the same way, working on projects that need immediate attention. Such a person might do well in a sales job that required travel, retail operations, or an entrepreneurial venture.

The "pacer," on the other hand, may be frustrated in a work environment that is chaotic and unstructured, where decisions are made on the spot. This type of person usually works best in a stable, thoughtful work culture with a broad and deep infrastructure. Of course, there are many exceptions, and people can learn to adapt, but we generally are happier when our personal traits mesh with our work culture and our coworkers' style of doing things.

Let's consider another set of personal characteristics. Karen is best described as ambitious and socially bold. She has an "ascendant" temperament, which means that she is strong-willed and resolute when she puts her mind to a task. She is also highly intelligent and confident, bolstered by a successful academic history, excellent performance reviews, and notable achievement. People like Karen usually are happiest when they are contributing meaningfully to their profession or company. The Karens of the world are focused and determined, and they have a high resolve to achieve their personal and professional objectives.

Another type of person, who measures high in conceptual ability and intelligence but low in drive (desire to achieve), may excel in a particular job but probably will not rise to the highest levels in the field. Often people with modest ambition place a higher value on achieving balance in their lives than on rising to the upper echelons of the career ladder. Success in the corporate world isn't the end-all and be-all for them.

Ask yourself these questions:
- Are you practical and down-to-earth, or do you tend to be imaginative and creative?
- How does this trait impact your daily work?
- Does your job allow you to express these traits?

In my practice I regularly administer diagnostic tests to identify my clients' key attributes, traits, and personal characteristics. One of these standardized tests, the Guilford-Zimmerman Temperament Survey, poses three hundred questions from which a profile is developed. For example, a high score on the General Activity/Energy scale indicates a person—let's call her Ann—who likes to be physically active and can sustain a vigorous work schedule easily. People with such a high energy level tend not to tire easily and may be bored in a job that doesn't allow a physical outlet.

Ann's score on the impulsiveness/rhathymia (easygoing, carefree behavior) scale also suggests that she is inclined toward action. This characteristic is fairly typical of retail store managers, plant managers, sales personnel, and other action-oriented professionals. Scientists, controllers, accountants, and others in professions that require a more cautious and restrained approach in making decisions would likely score at the other end of the scale.

The Guilford-Zimmerman Temperament Survey also measures emotional stability (Ann's high ranking shows that she doesn't get rattled easily) and interpersonal skills (another category where Ann scored high). Her test results indicate that Ann is tolerant and doesn't easily show her frustration. Finally, Ann's answers reveal a reasonably strong-willed person, who stands up for what she believes in and does not back down easily—traits necessary for someone in a fast-paced, highly competitive, aggressive job.

The 16 PF (Personality Factors) Test Profile, another measurement tool used in Core Themes work, constructs a person's profile by examining sixteen personality factors (*see Figure B on page 108*). The key findings show the client—we'll call him Mike—as being reserved and fairly serious-

FIGURE B

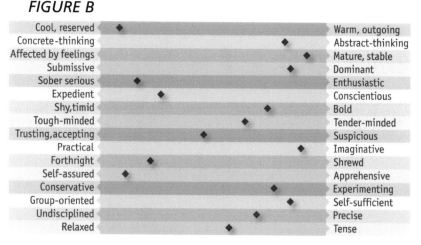

Cool, reserved	Warm, outgoing
Concrete-thinking	Abstract-thinking
Affected by feelings	Mature, stable
Submissive	Dominant
Sober serious	Enthusiastic
Expedient	Conscientious
Shy,timid	Bold
Tough-minded	Tender-minded
Trusting,accepting	Suspicious
Practical	Imaginative
Forthright	Shrewd
Self-assured	Apprehensive
Conservative	Experimenting
Group-oriented	Self-sufficient
Undisciplined	Precise
Relaxed	Tense

Note: Fig B is a representation only and not the official 16 PF Test Profile.

minded. He is competitive and assertive and demonstrates a willingness to take charge (bold, dominant). At the same time, he can be somewhat sensitive (tender-minded) and prefers more creative, conceptual activities (abstract-thinking, imaginative). Mike's other defining characteristics include being nontraditional and willing to change and try new things (experimenting, bold). He also tends to be independent (self-sufficient) and not easily influenced by other people (self-assured). Mike's profile clearly indicates that he prefers work that is intellectually challenging.

My Core Themes clients usually take a dozen or so standardized tests to determine everything from interests and skills to intellectual abilities and emotional intelligence. A thorough self-assessment of your personality and how it affects your work will provide valuable information that can aid you in your search for a fulfilling job. If you do decide to sign up for personality testing with a professional, here are a few things to keep in mind:

- The consultant who interprets your test results should have experience in the field and familiarity with the specific tests being administered. Ideally, he or she should have a background in psychometrics, which specializes in measuring and evaluating psychological differences.
- Ideally, the tests should be standardized and should have proven reliable over many years. Other assessment tools include questionnaires and surveys that may not be standardized tests but can be very useful when interpreted by an experienced professional.
- You should undergo a comprehensive battery of tests and questionnaires, not just one test. This will give you an overall view of the areas shown on Figure A (*pictured on page 98*).
- Test results should be examined and interpreted in the context of your personal life history and professional experiences.

MOTIVATIONAL PROFILE (UNDERLYING NEEDS)

Identifying your interests and motivations—why you do certain things—can provide another key to finding happiness and success. Ask yourself:

- What are your needs, interests, and underlying motives?
- Are you motivated by money, by the desire to help people, by both, or by something else?
- Do you need to have autonomy in your everyday dealings, or do you work best in a collaborative setting?

Think of your "needs" as being essential and your "wants" as being optional. For example, most of us require a means of transportation (a need). For many millions of us who work outside the home, this usually means an automobile. We have many options to choose from. Whether we drive a Mercedes (a want) or a less expensive Camry (also a want), the choice usually comes down to what we can afford. Regardless of which one you choose, the underlying requirement to get from home to work is a need.

Needs, then, are deeper than wants. It is important to identify our primary needs as they relate to our lives and work. Basically, needs drive much of our behavior. If we feel thirsty (a need), we reach for a glass of water to satisfy ourselves. If we are lonely, we may call a friend. To the extent that you meet your needs, you will be satisfied. If you don't, you will be unhappy and frustrated. For example, if you have a tremendous need to be successful yet you work in a shrinking company, you will eventually have to deal with your frustration.

Let's assume you have a high need for order and structure. This need is clearly manifested in your personal and professional life in the way you organize your home and your work space and in the way you perform tasks. You are the type of person who plans, organizes, and follows certain prescribed procedures. Imagine yourself working in a fast-paced, highly evolving business. You have little time to follow your normal routine, and as a result you find yourself frustrated by loose ends, messy coworkers, and stressful deadlines. You find it essential that your daily activities reflect your internal need for order and structure. Because your need for order is not satisfied, you are likely to be unhappy and less productive.

For those of you who are parents of small children, you have probably become experts at teaching your children the difference between needs and wants. Your toddler son frequently says, "I need this, Mommy!" You remind him that he already has three toys just like the one he is asking for.

Unfortunately, some adults continue to interchange the terms and that can sometimes be problematic. If you are chasing a want instead of an actual need, you may be spending a good deal of your energy going in the wrong direction. Now, there is nothing inherently wrong with desiring various things (wants), but it is important to understand the difference between that and needing something.

TV personality Jay Leno owns a large collection of antique automobiles and motorcycles. When he decides to add another expensive car to his collection, it qualifies as a want and not a need. Get the picture?

Let's look at another example. Suppose you have a need to be around people. You are sociable, friendly, and the nurturing type who genuinely likes people. Your company, however, values you for your technical skills and the expertise you bring to projects. You have little time to develop lasting relationships or mentor colleagues. You have ignored a need and as a result, something is missing in your work life.

When assessing my clients' motivations, I sometimes use the Edwards Personal Preference Index, which examines basic needs and motives. It's an interesting test because it can reveal a great deal about a person's underlying needs.

Let's look at a hypothetical profile of "Bill." Bill's most dominant needs are:

- Achievement 77%
- Exhibition 93%
- Dominance 91%
- Deference 75%
- Intraception 89%
- Aggression 97%

Bill's lowest needs are:
- Nurturance 1%
- Order 19%
- Affiliation 0%
- Endurance 3%

These results indicate that Bill is fairly ambitious and self-motivated (77 percent on the achievement scale). Complementing this is Bill's need to take charge and act decisively (dominance, 91 percent). He is prone to challenge others (97 percent on the aggression scale). His high score on the exhibition scale (93 percent) suggests that he is focused on results and likes the recognition that comes from his work.

These findings suggest that Bill is a strong-willed person. Given his drive level (achievement) and need to take charge (dominance), Bill would be happiest in a job and a company where he can advance. He will also function better around other self-motivated and ambitious colleagues. Bill's low scores in affiliation and nurturance suggest that he doesn't have a strong need to be around people, and if given the choice he is probably most comfortable working alone or with only a few coworkers.

You will be much happier in a job that allows you to act in accordance with your true motivations and interests. If your needs conflict with the requirements of your work, you may find yourself feeling unhappy and resentful. If your profile is like Bill's, for instance, it's not likely that you would be a good fit for a position as a nurse or an elementary school teacher. Those professions require people who are warm, caring, and nurturing.

Knowing your underlying needs makes it much easier to select a job where you can be happy. Knowing what you need is only part of the goal, however; you must also work to satisfy your needs. One of my clients came to me highly frustrated over his job, but he couldn't pinpoint the reason for his feelings. As the leader of a group of database analysts, he conducted research, crunched numbers, and reported findings to the president and other top executives of his company. After making his report, he went on to the next project.

After we discussed his work and his history, I administered a battery of assessment tests. The results proved to be very interesting. He had the ability to understand complex ideas (high conceptual ability), was extremely intelligent, and had superb cognitive powers. It was obvious that his work, which had become routine and repetitive, bored him. Like many competent professionals, he had outgrown his job, and his need for intellectual stimulation had gone unfulfilled for several years. What he really wanted was to be a member of the executive team, where he could make strategic decisions. Eventually, he resigned to take a job at a think tank organization.

This man's Core Themes work helped him gain a clearer perspective on his needs and career direction. At his new job, he exercises his intellectual strengths more fully, surrounded by people of similar talents and interests. It's an exciting moment when someone gains such insight and learns that satisfying one's needs can provide true fulfillment in both work and life. That's when a person takes control of his life and makes choices that are right for him.

Think about your needs:

- What are your most important needs, those "must-haves" that make your work interesting and challenging?
- How can you meet those needs at work?

PERSONAL AND PROFESSIONAL VALUES

One of the real keys to happiness is making sure that our work and our company follow the same personal values and principles that we do. Consider these questions about your values:

- What is most important to you? Honesty? Family? Integrity? Work ethic? Working with people you like? Believing in what you are doing?
- To what degree are any of these values critical for you to achieve real happiness in your life and work?

Being true to your values is essential to your happiness and well-being. Take the case of Bob, a highly successful, well-paid professional who had risen to the highest levels within his field. As senior vice president of marketing, Bob brought to his job a great deal of talent, expertise, and creative thinking. Ethical and honest, he believed that his customers deserved the best products available for the price. His former company based its success on providing high-quality products and customer service. Bob continued to hold onto those values when he accepted a promotion at a different company.

Intelligent, competent professionals sometimes disagree on business philosophy, strategies, and tactics. When this occurs, it can cause a breakdown in communication and collaboration, and the business can suffer as a result. Bob often shared his business philosophy with colleagues and the president of the company where he had transferred. It eventually became clear to Bob that they did not share his approach to business. He struggled with this issue for some time. His health began to decline, and he became anxious, preoccupied with the issue, and unable to concentrate on his job or his family.

Eventually, Bob made the difficult decision to leave the company. He walked away from a high-paying, prestigious position, but in his heart he knew he was doing the right thing for himself. Bob's decision to leave took a great deal of courage and was not done casually. However, he found himself amid a group of colleagues who did not share his business philosophy. He has never looked back.

Bob landed a position as president/CEO of a dynamic catalog company. As the top executive, he could now impart his strong personal and professional values without having to compromise. Bob was very successful in growing this company and for ten years was able to apply his experience, knowledge, and leadership without any serious challenges to his core values.

Almost as soon as he left his former position and in his ten years at the new company, Bob was virtually free of the types of stresses he felt in his old job. He and his family were in a much better place in all respects.

Peter is another executive who found himself at odds with his company's philosophy. He joined a growing high-tech company as vice president of marketing and sales with the understanding, based on a discussion with his soon-to-be boss, that his work week wouldn't often exceed fifty-five hours and that he would travel only 25 percent of the time. Those limits were important to Peter, the father of two young girls and the husband of a loving wife who had her own career to manage. In fact, the lack of time with his family had been the big motivation for Peter to seek a new job in the first place.

Once on board, Peter discovered that the company expected him to work sixty-five to seventy hours a week and travel even more than he had in his last job. Conveniently, his boss couldn't remember their previous conversation.

Although Peter liked his new job, the heavy work schedule ran him ragged, caused him stress, interfered with his fitness routine, and most important, prevented him from spending time at home with his family. His daughters missed him, and his wife had been forced to assume much more of the parenting role than the couple had agreed upon.

As time went on, Peter came to understand his need for balance—the need for a good job and a good home life—and he concluded that he didn't have a future at his new company. Being able to spend time with his family proved to be more important to him than success at work, which required an all-consuming effort. Eventually, Peter resigned from his position and landed a job with another company that placed a higher value on family and balance.

Every business culture is unique and is usually defined by the top leadership. The company where Peter originally worked was aggressive and growth-oriented. These goals were a good match for many workers at the company, but for Peter, his family and personal well-being were more important than his career.

Values can drive decisions. After much soul-searching, Steve, another client, determined that his most important Core Theme was integrity. In our many conversations, he consistently brought up examples of people he admired who had great integrity and a sense of honor—people who never went back on their word. He said he had always tried to live his life that way and to treat others with respect. Steve had no idea that his own integrity would soon be challenged.

As he conducted his job search, Steve came across an opportunity that he believed would give him a chance to prove himself as a leader and an executive. After several weeks of negotiation, Steve and his prospective employer accepted a verbal agreement on the terms of his employment. Three days before Steve was to start the job, he received an offer of a position with another company. The new offer would pay him double the salary of the other position and required little travel. This meant he could be home in the evenings with his family, and the extra money would enable him to build their vacation dream house on the lake. By anyone's measure, it was a great opportunity.

There was only one problem: the job he'd already accepted. Examining his Core Themes for the answer to his dilemma, Steve knew what he needed to do. He had given his word to the president of the first company, and although he had not signed a written contract, it didn't matter. As a person who based his entire value system on integrity, Steve kept his word and took the first position. There really was no other choice that met his ethical code. For Steve, it was critical that he live by his values. And that's what he did—he kept his integrity intact.

If we live and work according to our values, we will sleep a lot better at night. If we allow ourselves to become disconnected from them, we usually pay the consequences. Think about your own values and the role they play in your life:

- What are your primary values?
- How do your values affect your life?
- Your work?
- Your relationships?

INTEREST PROFILE

It is common for people to enter their career based on a strong interest or avocation. For example, a love of dogs may lead someone to attend veterinary college or become a veterinary technician. An interest in computers may develop into the study of computer programming. A natural aptitude for mechanical devices may deepen one's interest in mechanical engineering. A love of the outdoors may result in a career as an instructor with Outward Bound. An interest in children may inspire someone to major in child development or to become an elementary school teacher.

Our early interests and experiences often influence our initial career choices and our selection of academic courses. Felice was brought up in a family who appreciated the arts. At the tender age of seven, she already showed signs of creativity. Her parents frequently took her to art museums and private and public art galleries. Felice's parents and her art teacher encouraged her to develop her artist talents.

Throughout her school years Felice exhibited a passion for painting and the arts. As she approached college age, she researched schools with first-rate art programs. She majored in art and after graduation landed a teaching position in a private school. But it wasn't long before she became disillusioned and frustrated at not being able to teach in the manner she preferred.

This young, talented, and responsible woman had chosen a career based primarily on her strong love for and interest in the arts. She never really considered any other career direction and never received any advice or direction about other career possibilities. She chose a career in a field in which she had been immersed since childhood. But she never took the time to learn about herself and explore other career options.

Now, finding herself terribly unhappy and burned out, she feels trapped and stuck. Because being an art teacher is the only career she has ever known, she lacks confidence in her other abilities and has no idea what else she can do.

Felice is a classic example of someone who chose a career

based solely on interests and early life experiences. When she relied on her love of art to choose a career, however, she became frustrated and disillusioned. What happened?

Exploring your natural and learned interests is certainly an important part of the puzzle when figuring out what you want to do for your life's work. But it is only one piece of the puzzle. Most of us have many interests, which derive from all kinds of sources.

Perhaps when you were a child, your parents worked in academia, and you grew up in a home where books and reading materials were everywhere. From your earliest memories, your parents read to you and later encouraged you to read anything and everything. Consequently, you developed a strong interest in American history.

Or you grew up in a family business, a small engineering consulting business, run by your father and your grandfather. Maybe you worked at the local marina as a kid and acquired a love of boats and sailing. Perhaps you had a knack for working with children and spent your summers as a camp counselor, which led to a teaching career. Or growing up in the great outdoors led you to a career as a wildlife biologist.

One of the well-known standardized tests used to assess a person's interests is the Strong Interest Inventory Profile. The Strong profile combined with other assessment instruments is an excellent tool to measure a person's interests (not skills or abilities). It is very useful in helping people identify certain careers that are of interest and other careers that are of little or no interest.

The Strong profile features six categories: social, realistic, conventional, investigative, enterprising, and artistic. The categories are rated from low to very high, and each category provides a sampling of careers that reflect the category.

For example, test results showed that Amy, a thirty-year-old with a degree in accounting and nine years of experience in the insurance and energy industries, recorded high interests in the social and realistic categories. Among the careers within the social category are occupational therapist, registered nurse, recreation therapist, and physical therapist.

Amy's top five interest areas included health care services, protective services, taxes and accounting, the military (Amy had won a full ROTC scholarship to a prestigious college but had failed the physical), and counseling and helping. The areas of least interest to her included law and politics, public speaking, and entrepreneurship.

The information contained in the Strong report proved very useful in helping Amy sort out the reasons and motives behind her interest in certain categories and specific careers. Just because people have a strong interest in a career or activity doesn't necessarily mean they want to engage in that activity as their life's work. The fact that Amy showed a keen interest and curiosity about the health care field suggested that there were elements within that field that genuinely appealed to her. Where conversely, Amy had virtually no interest in the legal field or in owning her own business (Amy's other assessment data in addition to her personal history made it clear that she was averse to risk and valued security and stability above all else). Knowing the categories that interest you can often provide you with a place to start exploring.

As you think about and explore your future career, remember that it is vitally important to determine which interests, no matter how passionate you are about them, would make good hobbies and which would qualify as a potential vocation.

PUTTING IT ALL TOGETHER

Now it's time to evaluate the information that you've collected during your reflections about who you are, what your skills are, and what you value most. Honestly review what you have discovered in your self-interviews and assessments. Be open to insights and be prepared to confront obstacles.

The discovery process can be an enormous help in identifying your needs. Consider the case of Arlene, who worked in product development for a major retail company. She was young, smart, and in a fix. In fact, her employer was letting her go. On the surface, the problem seemed to be that she was not a team player. She seemed unmotivated, and her superiors considered her work to be lackluster.

An examination of her strengths and limitations showed a different picture, that of a young woman with extremely high analytical and conceptual abilities. She "got it" before anyone else did. Arlene was competitive, forthright, energetic, and strong-willed.

Arlene's Core Themes work revealed other strengths:
- She had a high need to investigate complex issues and act autonomously.
- She had a strong drive and an intense desire to achieve.
- She was willing to take charge of any situation.
- She was an independent thinker.
- She preferred work that was intellectually stimulating, varied, and creatively challenging.

The assessment also revealed Arlene's limitations. She often made up her mind too quickly, she became bored easily, and she wasn't especially collaborative with her peers.

Clearly, this young woman, who might have been a star

in another setting, worked in a job that didn't ask enough of her, and she was bored. Stifled by the mundane tasks expected of her, she felt trapped and unhappy, and neither she nor her employer fully understood why.

The results of Arlene's assessment have helped her understand what she needs in her next job. She knows that the work must be intellectually challenging and allow her to act independently if she is to succeed and feel satisfied. When we last spoke, she was looking for a way to satisfy her love of travel, gardening, and cooking with her need for creative expression, intellectual stimulation, and autonomy. Now that she has a clearer sense of direction, she will have a better chance of making the best decision for herself.

Consider, too, the case of Phil, a forty-two-year-old office manager for an accounting firm. Phil's financial and accounting background, plus his general business acumen, suited him well for running the firm's day-to-day operations, which allowed the partners to focus on their jobs. After thirteen years with the firm, Phil was at a crossroads. The company had begun making changes, including hiring a new general manager, which worried Phil, who had had the same boss for his entire career at the firm.

Phil went through the Core Themes program to sort out his feelings and thoughts and determine what his next steps should be. The information gathered from his personal and career history and test results was enlightening. The assessment showed Phil had above average skills at analytical and conceptual thinking. He excelled in math and the ability to use facts to solve problems. Phil focused on getting results and was willing to take charge. In all, he was a thoughtful and cautious decision maker who could take a tough stand when needed and who liked being around other people. The results also showed that Phil lacked basic marketing and sales skills, had a skeptical streak, and was not highly organized. He felt uncomfortable in an environment that was fast-changing or chaotic.

The knowledge of himself gained from the Core Themes program helped Phil resolve his career and life issues. He realized that his role at the firm was indeed a good fit for him and that he enjoyed the people, the work, and the culture. His skeptical nature caused him to worry and wonder if he could work with the new boss and continue to succeed at the firm. When he considered his Core Themes, however, Phil realized that his job fulfilled his requirements and satisfied his needs. In the end, he decided to remain with the firm. When he finally left the company five years later, he again turned to his Core Themes for guidance in choosing another position.

A deep examination of your life and work will provide insights about yourself that will lay the groundwork for identifying your Core Themes. Now let's explore what brings meaning and purpose to your life.

SIX

Phase 2: Finding Purpose and Meaning in Your Life

If you follow your bliss, you put yourself on a kind of track that has been there all the while, waiting for you, and the life that you ought to be living is the one you are living. Wherever you are—if you are following your bliss, you are enjoying that refreshment, that life within you, all the time.

—Joseph Campbell, author

Too many of us put life on automatic pilot. We pass our lives without much thought of how we are actually spending our time. Without probing into our hearts, we never identify what gives meaning and purpose to our lives. We get bogged down in the clutter of everyday trivia and never live life to the fullest.

Alicia, the young woman we met in Chapter 1, was well-educated and cultured, but she was confused and unfocused about which direction to follow in pursuing a career. She innately knew that there was more to her life than working in a laboratory in a major hospital, even though it was a job that matched her academic credentials. Something was missing.

As in the case of so many people, the clutter kept her trapped in a job that was going nowhere fast. Alicia eventually found her true passion and purpose, but not before she went through a series of probing exercises and reflection to gain clarity. Once she became clear about the path she truly wanted to follow, her clutter vanished.

The following exercises will help you discover what gives your life meaning and purpose. We'll start with Exercise 1.

EXERCISE 1: YOU'RE RICH, NOW WHAT?

Imagine for a moment that you're one of those extraordinarily lucky people who happen to choose the winning numbers in a giant lottery. After taxes, you receive a check for $30 million. Now you can live life the way you've always wanted to live it. What would you do? How would you pass the time now that you don't have to earn a paycheck?

Visit the candy store in your mind and browse through all the options that would make you happy. Remember, you don't need to worry about making money. Just think about the activities that satisfy you deep down in your soul.

The value of this exercise is to separate what you'd love to do from the need to make money. This allows you the freedom to explore your desires and the activities that would give your life meaning. Think carefully about your answers and write them down. Go into detail. What's so appealing about the activities you chose? How would they bring purpose and meaning to your life?

One of my clients, a university president, left the world of higher education and began searching for a new career. His first answer in this exercise was a bit surprising: he wanted to spend more time pursuing one of his passions, training Labrador retrievers.

That was a valuable insight for this man, whose working life until then had been spent in esoteric and intellectual pursuits. He seemed quite adamant in his response. Pushing him to think about his choice more deeply, I told him to consider day-to-day life as a dog trainer and what it would really be like for him.

When he came into my office for the next appointment, a smile brightened his face. "I know what you're doing," he said. Then, referring to his earlier decision, he acknowledged, "I could never do that." He had indeed thought about working with his beloved Labradors all day and had concluded that he would never find enough intellectual stimulation in that line of work to make him happy for long, much as he loved it as a hobby. He also concluded that he would miss being involved with people. My client eventually found a position in another field related to higher education. A new focus, not a change of career, fulfilled his needs.

It's important that we understand the distinction between an avocation and a vocation in choosing a career. The university president's avocation—his passion for the outdoors and for working with dogs—brought him relaxation and a great deal of personal satisfaction. He took great pleasure in seeing his charges develop into well-trained field dogs and handling them in field trials.

Like the president, each of us has hobbies and interests that could be turned into full-time careers. Before making such a choice, however, you will need to examine closely your motives in making the change, the abilities and skills necessary for the job, and whether you can support yourself. Most important, you need to make sure that your Core Themes match the activity or position you are considering.

One client, a former director of information technology for a wholesale company, had worked his way through college as an employee at a retail frame and print business. A serious student of art and artists, he derived much pleasure from the art world. After leaving the corporate world behind, he rediscovered his interest in art. At first he tried to sell artwork on his website. That venture failed. Eventually, he purchased an existing art and frame shop in an exclusive seaside community. Since his primary Core Theme is to be independent, the job fills that need. He is on his way toward achieving success at a career he loves, free from the demands of the corporate world.

This exercise usually produces a long list of activities and interests. For Todd, the unhappy school superintendent in Chapter 3, the list included:

"My wife and I would travel all over the country and around the world, touring and enjoying different cultures.

"We would live in a warmer climate during the winter.

"I would become active in church and civic organizations.

"I would give to charitable organizations.

"I would learn another language.

"I would develop my cooking skills.

"We would exercise more and eat a healthier diet.

"I would earn my doctorate."

A full list. In putting it together, Todd identified those things that really mattered to him—his love for his wife, his interest in people, and his desire to learn and have fun. None of it had anything to do with satisfying a school board or placating unhappy parents. This was Todd's wish list for a happy life, and it helped him see with new clarity that life held many interests for him.

The point of this exercise is not necessarily to help you decide what your next career will be. Todd, for instance, was unlikely to become a travel writer or a chef, even though he had interests in those fields. Like the would-be dog trainer, Todd eventually realized that an avocation isn't necessarily a good choice for a vocation. But the list helped him understand what made him happy. Cooking, for example, allowed him to be creative and relaxed and challenged him at the same time. When he finally settled on becoming a human resources director for a school district, the position incorporated several of his needs and interests: his interest in other people (if not foreign cultures), his need for creativity, and his desire for a challenging occupation.

Finding your true calling is a little more complicated than just deciding what you like and then doing it. It involves taking a deep look at your abilities, interests, values, needs, and skills. This exercise is one of the essential building blocks in identifying and defining your Core Themes. Your answers can help you recognize an unfulfilled need that any future career has to address if you are to be happy. The challenge you now face is to determine which of your choices are required for you to be happy.

One of my clients, a writer, told me that if he won the lottery he would learn Greek. I suggested he explore what that desire represented. Was learning Greek a passing interest, or was it a symbol of something deeper he needed to fulfill in order to be happy? Perhaps one of his Core Themes was lifelong learning, and studying Greek was only the tip of his unexplored passions.

Review your answers one by one. Ask yourself: Am I merely interested in these things, or are they a part of who I really am? There's a big difference. Many of us like to travel, but relatively few of us have to see the world in order to feel fulfilled. Those people see travel and the discovery of a broader world as something they simply have to do in this life, and for them travel is indeed a Core Theme. The former school president, on the other hand, loved working with dogs but upon deeper reflection saw the activity as a passionate hobby, not his life's work.

This first exercise often helps people realize that they are not doing the things that would make them happy, or that they are not doing them often enough. Money may not even be the issue. The writer did not need to be wealthy to learn Greek, but he needed to take the first step, perhaps signing up for a course at the university or buying a series of conversational tapes, if learning Greek was indeed important to him.

This exercise, then, is designed to get you thinking, to make you realize that you have interests and needs beyond what you are doing right now. It helps uncork your creativity and lets you fantasize about your desires, without tying those dreams to a paycheck. And it reinforces the point that money should flow from doing what you love to do.

Courage to Explore

The biggest obstacle to being happy in your life and work is not finding the courage to explore what you know is right for you. Changing your life can be scary, particularly when you don't have a clue what that change will be or where it will lead. All you know for certain is that you are unfulfilled and unhappy in your current profession.

So you stick with what is familiar and safe. But as many

of us have discovered from our life experiences, familiar and safe are not necessarily good things. We are creatures of habit; most of us follow the same routine every day. We settle in and become comfortable. We become complacent and no longer live our lives with the energy, motivation, and excitement of earlier years.

I frequently travel from my office in quiet Portland, Maine, to conduct business in nearby Massachusetts, which is famous for heavy traffic on its roadways. I often wonder when I pass other motorists if they woke up that morning with a sense of excitement about the day ahead or with a dread of facing the same challenges that confront them every day. How many years have they been driving the same roads? Are they thinking positive thoughts about their day or are they thinking about what they'll do after work?

Sometimes these day-to-day patterns are shattered by unexpected events that push us to make changes we know we need to make. Daniel's experience is a good example of this. Daniel, a forty-three-year-old financial professional we first met in the Introduction of this book, expected to be awarded the chief financial officer (CFO) position in his company. He believed that, after fourteen years with the company, he had earned the CFO position when his boss retired. When he did not win the position, he made changes that would have surprised him earlier in his career.

Daniel initially decided to go into the financial/accounting area because the intellectual challenge attracted him, and he loved the demanding aspects of the business world. Eventually, he rose to the second-highest level in his company as the controller. Daniel especially liked working with people and mentoring the younger financial professionals in the firm and those who directly reported to him. But there were aspects of the job he did not like. Daniel was by nature an easygoing guy and grew to hate the politics of the large corporate culture. He especially disliked the tension and negativity associated with certain colleagues as well as the changes in the company as a result of new leadership.

"I knew I wasn't totally satisfied with my profession and the company's direction," he said sometime after we had started to analyze his situation.

During the course of Daniel's self-evaluation work, a project he was supervising failed to meet the agreed-upon objectives. Even though circumstances beyond Daniel's control compromised the project, the president of the company severely criticized him. Daniel was upset that he was singled out as the primary reason for the project's failure and thought that the criticism was unfair. "I felt I deserved fairer treatment from my boss," he said. "Circumstances worked against me."

Daniel decided to delve into the self-evaluation process to learn more about himself and his values. He was a loving husband and the father of three children. He enjoyed traveling and learning about other cultures, and he was deeply spiritual. Assessment tests showed that Daniel was smart, analytical, and competitive. The results indicated a slightly low energy level, probably due to Daniel's unhappiness at the time. Daniel found one result particularly revealing—his strong need to lead, something he had done in other aspects of his life in the past, although less often in recent years. "As the controller, I did not have the opportunity to strategize and provide the level of leadership that I craved," he said. "These were the purview of my boss and other top executives."

When he saw the results of his tests, Daniel realized that he was most fulfilled when he could lead other people and not be bogged down with the day-to-day minutiae that consumed him on his job as controller. He uncovered more revelations during the second Core Themes exercise, designed to identify one's innermost values.

EXERCISE 2: THIRTY PLUS YEARS INTO THE FUTURE
Imagine yourself at the age of eighty or so. What would you like to have accomplished in your life? What do you want your life to have counted for?

This may be the most serious question you'll ever have to answer, for it gets to the point of your life: What were you put here to do, and did you do it? What is the purpose and meaning of your existence?

Put yourself in a contemplative mood. Find a quiet room, a comfortable chair, a favorite place, and really ponder what your thoughts might be at the age of seventy-five or eighty, when you are still in relatively good health, with your working life at an end. As you reflect on the past thirty or forty years of your career, write down your accomplishments and the meaning of each in your life.

Daniel answered the question without hesitation: "I would want to make a significant difference in improving people's lives." Just as interesting was what Daniel did not say. This hypothetical retiree did not see his biggest achievement as having been a highly successful CFO in a large, prestigious company. Even if he were to become a highly respected and well-compensated CFO, it would not have brought him fulfillment. "I realized that if I got to the end of my life and my biggest accomplishment was to have been a great corporate CFO, I wouldn't have been satisfied," he said.

Daniel's clear thinking about what mattered most to him gave him the courage to pursue his dream. He acknowledged that he had taken the wrong road. He was not living his passion—or as author Joseph Campbell put it, following his bliss. Once he had identified his Core Themes, Daniel knew he needed to change his career. He set out to explore his options, knowing of his need to make a positive and significant difference in people's lives.

In the following months, Daniel networked with friends and professional contacts in nonprofit businesses. He focused on organizations that were prominent in helping the poor, both nationally and internationally. His efforts led him to accept a position with a prestigious and well-established nonprofit organization whose mission was to aid the poorest people in rural areas of the country.

Daniel's experience teaches us a lesson: Give yourself permission to remove barriers and explore the what-ifs. Allow yourself to dream, and think about what really brings you pleasure and satisfaction. Achieving a greater sense of fulfillment in our careers becomes possible if we can identify what we really want.

The image of looking back at yourself from old age has a sobering effect. It reminds you that your days on earth are finite, and that someday, if you are lucky, you will be old. When you sit and consider your failures, your successes, and your legacies, you hope that your thoughts and memories will be wonderful ones without any serious regrets.

When I presented this exercise to one of my clients, an especially intelligent and thoughtful man in his mid-forties, he said, "Ray, what makes you think I have two weeks left to live, let alone thirty or forty years?" That's exactly the point of the exercise. Most of us do not know how long we will live. My guess is that, if you knew you had only a couple of weeks or months left, you would spend those last moments in a way that was most meaningful to you and your loved ones.

Too many of us waste precious time doing things we really don't consider all that meaningful. Perhaps every once in a while we need to remind ourselves that our life is limited and that we should not squander this precious gift.

What people do with this exercise often reveals a great deal about their deepest feelings and beliefs. Let's take a look at the responses of Todd, the unhappy school superintendent. At age seventy-five, what would he want to have accomplished?

"I would like to think that I was the best son, brother, uncle, son-in-law, brother-in-law, nephew, and friend I could be," he said. "More important, I would like to be the best husband I could be. I could only hope that I gave back more than I received.

"I would like to know that I was solid and unwavering in my faith in God and love of God. I would want to be sure that I lived my life with the morals, values, and beliefs that I hold dear.

"I would want to think that I was a good person, and that people knew I was worthy of their trust, love, friendship, and confidence.

"That my life counted for something, and that I made a difference in the world. That the world or a person was better off because of me."

These were Todd's most intimate thoughts. Distilling them into one list helped Todd form a clearer picture of the person he wanted (and needed) to be and get a better grasp on how far he had to go.

Your answers to this question lead to the most important part of this exercise. If you know what you'd like to accomplish in your life, what are you doing to achieve those goals?

If you want to be remembered as the best husband or

wife or parent possible, where do you stand on that score today? If you fight regularly with your wife, how is that helping you to be the great husband you say you'd like to be? If you want someday to say that you helped those who needed it, when will you start doing good things for people? If you want to achieve fame or prominence in your career, when will you start actively pursuing that?

You have to start now to become the person you want to be later in life. That's true in a personal sense, and it's true in your professional life. Too many of us live our lives thinking that we'll always have another chance to make things right. We'll start to improve tomorrow, not today.

This is an uncertain world, one in which life can be snatched away in an instant—a point made horrifyingly clear on that momentous morning on September 11, 2001, when terrorists attacked the World Trade Center and the Pentagon. What if you never get the chance to set your life straight or do the things you have always wanted to do? What if you never get a chance to see your wife or husband or mother again? What would you regret not having told them?

As I was driving to work one morning, I heard on the news that a sixty-nine-year-old man had been killed the night before by a drunk driver. The irony of this tragic story was that the victim had been heading home from his last day at work—in fact, from a farewell party hosted by his coworkers. My first emotion as I listened to this story was one of sadness, and I quickly said a prayer for the man who had been killed. The second thought that crossed my mind was that I hoped he was coming from a job that he had enjoyed. The story would be too sad to bear if this man had waited until retirement to begin his real life. One can easily imagine that he had so many things planned: travel with his wife or visits with his daughter and grandchildren in Seattle. Maybe he was just looking forward to peace and quiet. But he never made it home. Little did he know when he got up that morning to punch the clock for the last time that he would meet his destiny that day.

The obvious lesson from this tragedy is that the time to act is right now to do what we know we need to do. We may not have another day on earth, let alone another thirty years, to make things right.

The vision my client Marie, the psychologist whose story was detailed in Chapter 2, had of herself at seventy-five led directly to a reevaluation of her life. She saw herself as a happy woman with no regrets, in part because she had never valued a job more than she valued her family, friends, and herself. The Marie of the future had learned to make commitments, to forgive and be forgiven, to have fun and accept herself.

In doing the exercise, Marie was wise enough to see that she couldn't accomplish all those things if she stayed on her present course. She soon made changes in her life that fit better with her ultimate goals and Core Themes.

Indeed, this exercise can have life-altering consequences, as the experiences of Marie and Daniel suggest. It can, if performed with rigorous honesty, produce a sense of rebirth. Writing down your thoughts and then reflecting on their meaning can put you in touch with what is most important in your life.

Let's move deeper into your heart.

- Write down what you have learned about yourself from these exercises.
- What do your responses say about how you are living your life?

- Where are the gaps between what you are doing and what you would like to be doing?
- Now write down what you are willing to change to bring your life into better balance.

PURPOSE AND MEANING

It seems that the first thing people do when they win the lottery or gain millions overnight is to leave their jobs. What does this say about how satisfied people are in their professions? It suggests that their jobs are simply a means to an end, a way to pay the mortgage and put food on the table.

Think of the dentist who has spent twenty years filling cavities and performing root canals. Is she still in her career because she is challenged by the work and loves helping her patients, or does it have more to do with making enough money to support a comfortable lifestyle? Is she, like many professionals, feeling stuck?

Life is not simply about working and making money. It's about achieving happiness and fulfillment in ways that are right for you. It's also about being fully accountable, not only for your performance but for the way you are living your life. In other words, you need to give your life and your job the best you have to offer. If you can no longer commit to that, it may be time to reflect on what really matters to you and your loved ones.

Your work has to mean something, and it has to provide something far deeper than a paycheck. Purpose and meaning are everything. Why do teachers work so hard for so little money? Why do nurses perform unpleasant tasks when they could make more money doing something else? Why do poets keep writing even though they're struggling to pay the rent? Why do successful executives and celebrities continue to work so hard when they have more money than they could spend in ten lifetimes? They do it because they find purpose in their callings, and that in turn provides meaning for their lives.

Patti was twenty-eight when she sought my help in late 2001. She had spent the past seven years earning a small fortune on Wall Street. When she came to my office in Maine for the first time, she was only one year away from never having to work again. Intelligent and with common sense far beyond her years, she said the one thing missing in her life was purpose and meaning in her career. She wanted to do something that would benefit society, not just herself and her clients. She had performed extremely well at her work, which had provided her with a lucrative income, but she knew in her heart that her career did not reflect her true values and interests.

Terrorists had demolished the twin towers of the World Trade Center in New York City only two months before our meeting. The tragedy had filled Patti with fear and forced her to reevaluate her life. Her unease over the state of the world became evident when Patti reached into her briefcase and pulled out a bottle of Cipro, the antibiotic used to treat anthrax, and a gas mask. I pointed to my tattered but dependable L.L. Bean canvas bag behind my desk. It held work documents, a dictation recorder, and maybe an overripe banana. What a contrast! Patti wanted what she believed I had—peace of mind and a slower pace. Most of all she wanted to find real meaning in her life, in a setting where random violence wasn't an issue.

The events of September 11, 2001, caused many people like Patti to weigh their values and examine more closely how they were spending their lives. One can see evidence of the search for meaning everywhere, even on the sports pages. When Michael Jordan, the great Chicago Bulls basketball player, returned to his beloved sport after a few years of retirement, I wondered why. The answer, I concluded, was that Jordan hadn't yet found real meaning and purpose outside of basketball.

Mr. Jordan belongs to the same club you do—that group of people who need to wake up each morning looking forward to a soul-satisfying activity. His challenge, and yours, is to discover that special purpose that elicits passion and excitement.

It's common to experience real fulfillment early in a career but then gradually lose it. Joanna spent more than twenty years as a human resource professional, mostly in banking and finance. As an HR director, she was successful, challenged, and fulfilled. Eventually, though, her work life went sour, and she struggled for the last two years of her employment. She endured many days when she could barely muster enough energy to show up at the office. What happened?

Joanna had entered the field because she enjoyed helping people and because she found the work interesting. She advanced quickly. Perhaps most important, she was always learning and growing, both professionally and personally. That provided her with the motivation she needed.

Joanna became less enchanted with her employer as consolidations and mergers brought more and more layoffs. Suddenly, it seemed, she was spending most of her time planning how to downsize the company. It pained her to see so many hardworking employees lose their jobs. Long gone were the opportunities for growth and the projects she so loved. She no longer found an outlet for her creative talents and believed her values were no longer compatible with those of the organization that employed her. It was time to change, but to what and where?

Joanna's reassessment eventually led her to take charge of her life and make choices in line with her true values and interests. She accepted a position with a nonprofit organization that put her in charge of creating and overseeing fund-raising campaigns for her employer. She experienced enormous inner peace and satisfaction from using her creative talents at the new job. Joanna's excellent people skills, honed over many years in her human resources job, her ability to make presentations to diverse groups, and her organizational skills fit perfectly with her new position.

She loved the notion of working for a nonprofit organization, where she could give of herself in a personal way. She earned less money than on her old job and lost her association with a prestigious bank. But the trade-offs were well worth it. She was now reenergized and passionate about the mission of the organization for which she worked. Instead of coming home to her husband each night complaining about her job and suffering from migraines, she now ended the day feeling positive about her accomplishments. The migraines disappeared, and her husband was much happier, as well.

Perhaps the most important lesson that Joanna learned was that she could choose to be happy—that she didn't need to remain in a job that held no real meaning for her. She assumed control of her life, and it felt good.

None of us wants to go through life with regrets. Of course, most of us would probably change some things about our life if we could roll back the clock. Maybe you regret never finishing your doctorate or never rafting the Colorado River. What happened to your idea of opening a crafts store in that beautiful little town in Vermont?

There are a million reasons why we don't do things we later wished we had. The biggest reason in almost every case is that we weren't willing to take the necessary risks. Nevertheless, taking risks is often the only way to get what you want in life. Growth comes from forcing yourself to stretch a bit. It could be as simple (or as complicated) as making a commitment to yourself to run your first 10K race a few months from now. Or writing your first article for the local newspaper. Or, for those of you who fear flying but love the study of other cultures, finally getting up the courage to confront your fears. If you do, a year later you may find yourself taking pictures of a Massai tribe in Kenya. What wonderful memories to take with you into your old age, all because you took a risk!

Some time ago, when I was an active therapist, I was invited to speak to a group of women who had one thing in common—they were all widows. As I listened to each woman tell her personal story, it struck me how they all shared feelings of loss and grief as if their husbands had died yesterday. The irony was that most had lost their husbands fifteen, twenty, or even thirty years before. Most of the women were now in their seventies. None had remarried; each had continued to feel depressed and to act as if life had cheated her. These women were clearly stuck and unwilling to take risks. For them, it was safer to remain single and miserable than to seek out new relationships. Getting involved in a new relationship would present new and different challenges that they did not want to tackle.

Although I respected their right to make their own choices, I felt sad that they had chosen to reject what life could have offered them and what they in turn might have been able to give back to others.

In his book *The Age of Unreason*, British writer Charles Handy describes the states of continuity and discontinuity. We are in a state of continuity when life is going well for us.

For example, we have a successful career, we're healthy and enjoy an active life, our company is doing well financially and paying generous bonuses. We are in a state of discontinuity when life turns sour: we suddenly have lost our job or become seriously ill or lost money in the stock market, or illness has struck a loved one.

The challenge for those in discontinuity at work is to get back on track by taking charge of life and doing what is necessary to have a happy and more fulfilling career. The choice is yours. I've always admired the men and women who decide not to allow their physical disabilities keep them from accomplishing extraordinary achievements. Every April, for example, a group of exceptional men and women with physical challenges compete in the Boston Marathon. Others climb Mt. Everest. Whatever their challenge, these brave people do not succumb to discontinuity in their lives, but choose instead to forge ahead. Doing that can be risky, but we can determine how much risk we should take by knowing ourselves thoroughly—to know what's most important to our well-being and satisfaction in life. And knowing ourselves can come only from careful self-examination and reflection.

I've worked with many men who tell me they would leave their jobs in a heartbeat to teach young children in public school if the pay were better. Instead of making a career change, they coach soccer or baseball, just for the love of working with kids. Instinctively these people know their Core Themes center on a need to counsel, teach, and influence young minds. Unfortunately, most of these men choose a line of work that doesn't provide that satisfaction and that doesn't fulfill their needs. They feel trapped not just by the money but by the investment they have already made in their jobs.

Gregory had worked hard to become vice president of

national sales for a fast-growing advertising agency. At thirty-six, he was well on his way to earning the high income and the status he had sought for the last twelve years. Nevertheless, he began losing interest in the business and had become weary of the constant travel. It eventually became clear that Gregory felt a strong need to do something of greater value than just making his company more profitable. He had chosen the fast-paced and exciting advertising business because of his desire to channel his drive and energy in an industry that could pay big dividends professionally and financially.

The job Gregory really craved, it turned out, was athletic director for a high school or small college. He even interviewed for a graduate program for athletic directors. But with two little girls at home and a wife about to make a big change in her career, Gregory chose not to walk away from his high paycheck. Instead, based on what he had learned about himself, Gregory decided to transfer to another division within his company. The change allowed him to spend more time with his family and devote more time to coaching kids. By working out a compromise, he was able to continue to earn high wages while filling his need to mentor children outside of work—all with less anxiety and stress. Perfect? No. But better by far than his previous unfulfilling situation.

TIME'S A-WASTING

If you are dissatisfied with how you spend your days at work, you are wasting precious time. What a terrible idea that is! Life passes too quickly to waste even one day. It seems like yesterday when you couldn't wait to reach your twenty-first birthday. Now, at thirty-six, you look back at your twenties and wonder where they went. The same phenomenon exists at each stage of life. Before you know it, your daughter, the little girl you took to her first day of kindergarten, is thirty-one and has a job in the big city. Where do the years go? *Don't let your life get so far down the road before you decide to change course. Now is the time to decide what is really important to you and to act on that decision.*

For many years I told my business partner, Sebastian G. Milardo, that I was going to get back into fly-fishing, a sport I loved to do in my younger days. Work, commitments, and other roadblocks kept me from pursuing this particular passion. My partner, fed up with hearing me bellyache about wanting to fly-fish and never doing it, presented me with a brand-new fly-rod and reel from L.L. Bean for my birthday. I thanked him for his thoughtfulness, but for a full year that fly-rod outfit took up residence in a corner of my bedroom. How quickly the year passed. In fact, the realization of the quick passage of time finally pushed me into taking that fishing equipment and using it. Since then, my son and I have enjoyed wonderful days together on some of the most beautiful rivers in Montana, Wyoming, and New Mexico. I am grateful that I have the memories of these experiences with someone I love so dearly. My partner's gift provided exactly the push I needed.

What push do you need to reexamine your life and find those deeply buried Core Themes that you need to satisfy? How long before you choose happiness and fulfillment?

SEVEN

Phase 3: Identifying Your Core Themes

*Core Themes—those unique values, needs,
and interests that define you personally
and professionally.*

Phase 3 begins with a list of your Core Themes, in order of importance to you. Your first draft is likely to be general, somewhat broad, and lacking specificity and clarity. It typically takes two to three drafts to produce your final list of Core Themes. Think of constructing your list as if you were a skilled wood carver creating a life-sized drake (male) mallard duck. With your special carving tools, you begin to whittle away at a block of wood. Gradually, the block begins to take the general shape of a duck, but it requires many more hours before the duck has all the characteristics of a mallard. Even when you can identify the duck as a mallard, it isn't until you paint the beak a bright yellow and the head a striking green color that it becomes clear that your mallard is a drake and not a hen.

So be patient as you explore the various elements that will guide you in creating your unique list of Core Themes. As you create your first draft, let's review the critical data you have learned about yourself.

Let's start with what you learned about yourself as you relived your personal history. Thinking back on your personal and professional development, recall the people (parents, siblings, teachers, coaches, bosses, friends, family members) who have influenced your life and the decisions you made. Consider the events and situations you have experienced, such as traveling to a foreign country, having been a competitive skater as a child, having grown up in a deeply religious family, or facing the death of your beloved dog. The people, events, and situations unique to you helped to shape the person you have become.

If you are like most of my clients, you may have overlooked these shaping influences and perhaps have never really given much thought to how they played a role in your beliefs, values, and interests and the decisions you made with respect to your career choice.

As an example of how powerful one's family experiences can be, let's look at the life and career of Sarah, a music director at a small university. Sarah grew up loving music. Her natural talent for singing developed further as she participated in local choral groups and studied with various music instructors. She graduated from a prestigious university with a major in music theory.

Sarah's family valued education, accountability, achievement, and a strong work ethic. As she matured personally and professionally, she accepted and lived by these values as she progressed through college and became a choral director.

Think about the *knowledge* and *expertise* that you have

acquired from both your personal and professional life experiences. What particular areas of knowledge still excite and interest you? Identify areas of expertise that you still enjoy learning about. Don't limit your thoughts to what you have learned in your profession. Think about activities and projects you have participated in within your community, church, school, and other venues.

Based on your previous work or academic experiences, what type of work environment suits you best? Do you like working in a large company with a well-developed infrastructure or do you prefer a more entrepreneurial work culture with few defined rules and little structure? Do you prefer a business that makes products or one that is service-oriented? Do you prefer a traditional business or one that is always in a state of transition? These and many other questions need to be explored as you think through your potential Core Themes.

What about your *personal requirements*, such as your need to be mentored or coached by experienced managers? Or do you prefer a high degree of autonomy in your job? Do you need to be intellectually stimulated and if so to what degree? Do you get a big kick out of producing tangible, concrete results?

To what degree do you require interpersonal relationships at work? Or do you prefer to work privately with limited contact with coworkers? If you are an extravert, you may not like working in a cubicle doing technical work and having little social interaction with your peers. On the other hand, if you are an introvert, meetings with coworkers may frustrate you as unnecessary distractions that interfere with your focus on your job.

Do you have a strong need for order and organization? If you do, a fast-paced, entrepreneurial work culture may frustrate and distract you. If you thrive under chaotic conditions, you may enjoy the creative energy that flows from such a business culture.

A person of high integrity may become despondent in a business that focuses on profits at the expense of quality. How important is integrity in your life and is this a Core Theme? If the leaders of your company do not honor their word, will you lose respect for them and be miserable at work as a result?

If you are an ambitious career professional, you will do better in a business that is growth-oriented and has a history of providing opportunities for their employees to advance. If one of your Core Themes is the need to achieve and do things of importance in your life, then you are best served by carefully choosing a company with a reputation for encouraging employees with high potential.

But perhaps you desire a balance between work and personal lifestyle. You may have a strong work ethic, but you don't want to have work consume your life. If this is the case, you need to examine carefully the business culture, the expectations of the job, and the personality and demands of your prospective boss to make sure they provide you with enough flexibility to have a full home life.

One's needs can change over time as a result of various factors affecting your life. For example, a young and ambitious woman executive becomes a mother for the first time. Suddenly, her priorities shift from climbing the corporate ladder to wanting to spend time with her child. No longer is she as excited at the prospect of traveling overseas for days or weeks at a time or putting in late hours at the office. Your personal needs and values play a key role in identifying your unique Core Themes.

As you construct your draft, consider your *accomplishments* and *achievements* in your personal and professional history. As an example, Sarah, the music director, had achieved much in her young life, both academically and professionally. One of her Core Themes—her ability to be creative—helped her reach those goals. Whether she remains in the music world or changes her career, she will always have the need to exercise her creative side in whatever she does. A person's Core Themes remain constant throughout one's life even when the external circumstances change.

List all of your achievements, no matter how small or insignificant you think they are. Then review them to see if they have common threads running through them. You may have relied on intellectual reasoning or creativity to accomplish your goals; or perhaps the achievements were the result of your ability to influence or your leadership skills or your expertise in strategic thinking.

Another common Core Theme focuses on your *geographic location*. For example, some people prefer a rural environment. They want to be close to nature: the ocean, the mountains, a farm, or a fishing hole. If a person's happiness depends on the availability of artistic resources—theater, art museums, and art galleries—then a city may be the right place to settle.

Remember, a Core Theme is what you consider to be an essential element to have a happy and successful life and career. A Core Theme isn't only about a job; it is about how you want to live your life.

What are some of your lifestyle choices? If you have an active family requiring close supervision, you may choose a company nearby to avoid a long commute from home to office. Or you may accept a position that requires you to live apart from your family during the workweek. This option allows the children to attend familiar schools and avoids relocating the family.

Being close to and responsible for elderly parents may limit your career opportunities. But if your Core Theme is defined as being accessible to your aging parents, then you make your career decisions accordingly.

A client of mine has an autistic teenager, which requires that he consider opportunities only within a certain distance from his home. He and his wife share equally the responsibility of caring for their child. This executive could have many more career options if he did not have a child with special needs. But in his case, his family and his child are his primary Core Themes.

Do you like to be involved in your community? Perhaps your passion is improving the quality of the school system or being a member of the local United Way campaign or serving in a leadership role in your church? Any of these strong interests can affect your career direction.

The professional who is passionate about his or her personal health may choose a career that allows time to train daily for a marathon or a bikeathon. Alternatively, a health-oriented person may choose to work in the area or at home to reduce commuting time that can be spent playing tennis, running, swimming, or working out at the local fitness center.

As you can see, not all Core Themes are directly related to your job, but they do influence where you work and the decisions you make about what you do.

One of my clients determined that balancing time equitably between work and family was essential to his achieving happiness and success in his life and his career. As he stated, "I have a strong desire to spend quality time with my family without compromising my professional standards. Similarly, I have a strong desire to perform at a high level professionally, but I don't want this to impede my ability to spend quality time with my family. The balance issue will be a constant struggle for me, as it is for many."

If you are to have a life and a career that bring you real happiness and success, not just occasionally, but every day, you must identify and describe the values, needs, and interests that define you as a person—your unique Core Themes. Then you must make a commitment to let your Core Themes guide you in making your career decisions.

As an example, you rely on a set of values, morals, and principles in your personal relationship with your spouse, partner, or children. These guidelines set the tone of the relationship and help develop trust, love, and mutual commitment. If any of these core values are breached—for instance, one partner in a marriage has an illicit affair—the trust between the couple is undermined and the relationship will suffer. Similarly, if you allow your Core Themes to be compromised, you risk your sense of well-being and happiness at work.

Like the values in a personal relationship, Core Themes are limited to a handful. These are the "must haves" you need to find continuous enjoyment and satisfaction in your career, the sense of purpose and meaning that brings fulfillment and validation.

One of the challenges in determining your Core Themes is differentiating between a strong interest (an avocation) and an element that is essential to your happiness (a Core Theme). For example, being an avid skier doesn't necessarily mean that you would be happy teaching skiing or owning a ski resort. Or being an expert in American history may not indicate a desire to teach the subject at the local university.

However, there is great value in examining why American history interests you. In doing so, you may discover certain elements that will lead you to your Core Themes.

IDENTIFYING POTENTIAL CORE THEMES
The following exercise will help you to hone each of your potential Core Themes:
- Define and clarify the meaning of each potential Core Theme. Be specific.
- Describe why each Core Theme is important to you.
- Identify how the Core Theme ties into potential professional opportunities.
- How you would feel if that Core Theme were missing in your life/career?

Let's take a close look at Michelle's Core Themes and see how she was able to clarify and hone them by responding to the exercise above.

Michelle
Core Theme 1: Strategic/Broad/Conceptual Thinking
What it means:
- Being able to solve problems on a broader scale.
- Bringing together information and trends across a broad spectrum and then finding the strategy that has the broadest impact.
- Finding strategies that break new ground or have the potential to become a leader in the market or both.
- Designing or creating scenarios that solve problems or capitalize on opportunities. Mostly my interest is in conceptual design, which is the bridge between the problem/opportunity and engineering.

Why this is important to me:
- I get energized thinking about the possibility to do something that will have a big and lasting impact.
- People are on the planet for only a short time. Why not use the time wisely and do things that can really make a difference?
- I don't like hearing that "it can't be done."
- I've always liked to create things and to know how things work. Knowing how things work is important to me because I can then apply that knowledge in new contexts.
- It's energizing to create something that didn't exist before. I feel I've accomplished something.

Professional implications:
- Operational jobs—ones that involve keeping the current state running smoothly—don't interest me. I know what to expect from operational functions and would ensure that new ideas are injected to be sure the operation is running at its best, but actually running an operational function on a day in, day out basis would leave me uninspired.
- Need to work with other people who have these same skills or appreciate them.
- If I were in a senior position that included an operational function, I would be sure to have the best ops manager possible in place to run that function so I could focus on more strategic/directional matters.
- My need to be part of design can be manifested in many different ways. It can involve designing something physical or designing a process, policy, or even a mission or strategy.

- Ideally, I would work for a company that designs a physical product that I find interesting. This doesn't mean I need to be actually designing that product, but just being part of it in some way is rewarding.

How would I feel if this were missing?
- Not very good. I need some element of strategic/conceptual thinking in any job I assume. Ideally, it's a big part of the job.
- I think this Core Theme is truly core.
- Overall, I do need to be playing a leadership role in creating new things.
- I don't need to be actually designing or engineering the thing. I could just be setting the context within which design must happen, then letting a team of people do their thing.
- The part about working for a company that designs a cool product is ideal, but not required.

Core Theme 2: Change
What it means:
- Being in an environment where change is embraced as a good thing.
- Not change for change's sake, but change to improve things, to be a leader versus a follower.
- Acknowledging that the world is always changing, and while some things remain the same, other things present new opportunities that must be grasped or you'll fall behind.
- Acknowledging that we're always learning. If you think you know it all, you've just taken yourself out of the game.

Why this is important to me:
- This ties into the strategic thinking Core Theme. It energizes me to think that we don't have everything figured out. That as we learn new things, as society changes, we must adapt. All of this creates opportunity that can be grasped by the willing, allowing one to differentiate and lead.
- Without change, a person is destined to follow, which starts to feel the same to me as running an operational function. Just following instructions and making sure the job is done well. Boring.

Professional implications:
- I need to work in a company and a field that embrace change, ideally seeing change as a requirement for success.
- I need to be sure I can put in place solid functions to execute changes successfully. Otherwise it's all for naught.

How would I feel if this were missing?
- In the long run, not very good.
- At the onset, it probably wouldn't impact me as much, since I would be learning about the new job. But once I mastered that, I would need to have the ability to change things to improve it. If there weren't acceptance of change, I would get bored quickly.

Core Theme 3: Develop/Help/Interact with People
What it means:
- Helping people learn about themselves. Drawing out their strengths and helping them acknowledge their opportunities so they can change/improve.

Why this is important to me:
- In the end, people make things happen. A company's biggest successes and obstacles come from the people in the organization.
- The human element is the most complex. It's fascinating to learn about it and figure out how to positively intervene to help someone get more happiness out of life.
- I really enjoy getting to know people. What's so cool is that everyone is unique.
- People are a source of humor, which is necessary for me to maintain balance.

Professional implications:
- My job has to involve working with people, leading them, which gives me a better opportunity to be in a position to develop their strengths and help them in other ways.
- Ideally, I want to work in a company that embraces the power of the human element. This would provide me the most latitude to grow and develop others, as well as myself.

How would I feel if this were missing?
- If it were completely absent, it would feel as though my work had no deeper meaning. It would feel somewhat superficial and possibly self-centered.
- Working with people and helping them makes me feel as though I'm giving something back.
- However, I can make do in a situation where the company isn't necessarily 100 percent behind development of people. There's a certain amount of development I

can do on my own in this realm without corporate support.

Core Theme 4: Financial Success
What it means:
- First, to work for a company that is financially successful (clean balance sheet, productive profit and loss). In the end, businesses have to make money to succeed.
- Second, to be personally financially successful.

Why this is important to me:
- I'm not one to amass a lot of money just so I can count my coins. I don't need a big house or expensive car to point at as a source of pride. For me, it's about having the means to experience new things and enjoy life, for both myself and my family. We like boating. We like to travel. I really have enjoyed learning to ride a motorcycle. I love woodworking. All of these things take money.
- I like to be prepared for difficult times.
- I would like to be able to retire comfortably.

Professional implications:
- My career choice needs to provide a decent level of income to achieve the goals listed above.

How would I feel if this were missing?
- I think I would feel very limited in my lifestyle.

Core Theme 5: Living in a Place Where I Can Easily Enjoy the Outdoors

What it means:

- I need to have ready access to the outdoors: oceans, lakes, mountains, and other natural resources.

Why this is important to me:

- The outdoors invigorates me. Its beauty can't be matched by anything man-made. It stimulates all of my senses and helps me think more clearly.

Professional implications:

- I don't think my profession necessarily has to be outdoors-oriented. It would be nice, but it's not a requirement.
- However, my profession would need to offer me the time to be outdoors. Example, I couldn't work in a city job seven days a week, with no chance to escape to the outdoors.

How would I feel if this were missing?

- Over time, it would affect my health and well-being.

Core Theme 6: Customer Service/Corporate Ethics

What it means:

- It means that the company I work for should be concerned about doing the "right" thing.
- Doing the right thing also applies to how customers and employees are treated.

Why this is important to me:
- I'm a values-based person. I couldn't sleep at night if I thought the company I worked for was knowingly cheating people, either customers or employees.
- Much like Jon Huntsman (author of *Winners Never Cheat*), I don't see this as being in conflict with being a tough negotiator. There are things you have to do to protect your personal interests or that of the business. However, I never see a situation where lying to people or cheating them is the best way to approach that. There's always a morally correct path.

Professional implications:
- Need to work for an ethical company, one committed to true customer service and respect for employees.

How would I feel if this were missing?
- As if I were taking an easy but corrupt path to service my own personal needs.

Core Theme 7: Independence
What it means:
- Having the latitude to make decisions.
- Being trusted to make decisions in the company's best interest, knowing that I'll learn from any mistakes.
- Need to have things make sense to me. I generally can't accept something verbatim without taking the time to understand it and know how I feel about it.

Why this is important to me:
- I don't mind selling ideas and concepts up the chain and laterally to get approval. It's part of any business

reality. However, if all decisions have to be vetted laterally and vertically, I get bored with the bureaucracy. I also begin to feel as if I'm not really doing anything, just following instructions.

- I don't think people (including myself) can truly learn if they're not accountable for the results of their own decisions, good and bad.
- The need for me to process things internally will never go away. However, I do "pick my battles" and have fully supported things with which I didn't agree.

Professional implications:
- Need to find a company that provides a reasonable amount of delegation.

How would I feel if this were missing?
- As though I'm not offering as much as I could.
- As though I'm not learning as much as I could.
- I would get frustrated and bored.

Answering these four questions for each potential Core Theme accomplishes a couple of goals. It forces you to think more deeply about the potential Core Theme and consequently helps you to distinguish your true Core Themes from other values, interests, and needs that are less important to you. Remember, any Core Theme that survives this exercise is going to be essential to your state of happiness and success. Core Themes are not incidental or optional!

Because you will list your Core Themes in order of importance, you will know which ones you need to focus on as you pursue a career and make critical decisions that can impact your life for years to come.

Here are a few other examples of Core Themes: Jim put Julie at the top of his list because she was a primary part of his life. He also included his relationship with God as being an important Core Theme. David, on the other hand, listed compassion as his top Core Theme, with integrity and autonomy also high on the list.

TESTING YOUR CORE THEMES

Once you are satisfied that you have a solid list of your "must have" Core Themes, it is time to involve your loved ones in the process. In this exercise, you will discuss each Core Theme on your list with someone (or several people) you love and trust. The goal is to describe each Core Theme in terms your loved one will understand and explain why you chose it and what it means to you. If your Core Themes are valid and your loved one knows you well, he or she can verify that the list truly represents your values, needs, and interests.

During this process, loved ones almost always ask questions, which forces you to clarify or expand on your Core Themes. Sometimes feedback from loved ones can bring you insight which alters your Core Themes or changes their ranking of importance.

When clients and their loved ones meet in my office, I see the positive effects of having someone confirm the list of Core Themes. It gives clients confidence in the results of all those long hours and hard work and encourages them to test their Core Themes in the real world.

Another important reason for including loved ones in this phase is that they must be fully supportive if their family member or friend is to be successful in following his or her Core Themes. Without such support, a person may find it difficult indeed to initiate changes affecting family members or others. The quest to follow one's Core Themes well could be delayed or quashed.

Remember Daniel, the corporate controller who discovered his Core Themes centered around helping the poor? Although his new position with a nonprofit organization did much to satisfy his Core Themes, Daniel's innermost desire was to help people living in the world's poorest countries. When he told his otherwise supportive wife, Joan, that one of his Core Themes was to work in an undeveloped country, she quickly expressed her reservations, given the fact that they had three young children. Daniel agreed to put that Core Theme aside temporarily. Fast forward eight years, and Daniel and Joan now live and work in one of the poorest countries on the planet. It took awhile, but Daniel finally fulfilled his most deeply held Core Theme.

In our life and work, we sometimes face challenges to our values, morals, and principles. We may be tempted to compromise our own rules. The same is true of our Core Themes. As you pursue your career, you may be faced with choices that do not align with your Core Themes. For example, if one of your Core Themes is a need for autonomy and independence and you accept a fabulous position that places you at the mercy of a "micro-manager," you will eventually become frustrated. You rationalize that, because of the high salary and other benefits (clutter), you can tolerate a boss who has a reputation for being extremely demanding and overly controlling. Sooner or later, though, you will have to deal with the consequences of your compromise—frustration, irritability, anger, and the stress that comes when you are not living your true values.

Our inner selves remain remarkably constant throughout life. Core Themes are forever. They represent the things you truly value, and those things don't change.

EIGHT

Phase 4: Using Core Themes to Find the Right Job

Remember, it is not just a question of what you **can** *do, but what you really* **want** *to do with your life.*

Now that you have identified your unique Core Themes—the elements you need for happiness and fulfillment in your career—it is time to put them into action. However, there is one more exercise you need to do before you develop your career search plan. The exercise is designed to identify the skills and strengths that make you marketable to prospective employers.

You are going to do what I call a "brain dump." It goes like this: make a list of all the qualities and skills you possess that apply to each of the following categories. You may use entries in more than one category.

The categories with examples are as follows:

Abilities & Aptitudes
- Strategic planning
- IT/business relationship management
- Financial management
- Broad conceptual thinking
- Excellent verbal and writing abilities
- High analytical aptitude

Personal Profile/Traits
- Bold, assertive
- Innovative
- Inquisitive
- Persuasive, willful
- Personable, cooperative

Experience
- Established progressive information architecture
- Led development of a business intelligence strategy
- High school history teacher
- Home improvements
- Led disaster/crisis debriefing teams
- Extensive travel to more than thirty-five countries

Knowledge & Skills
- Curriculum development
- Project management
- Public speaking
- Current events/literature/history
- Leadership of problem solving meetings
- Programming
- Financial budgeting

Values

- Direct but respectful approach
- Belief that people are a company's most important asset
- High integrity and honesty
- Aesthetic beauty
- Strong work ethic
- Customer service

Interests (personal & professional)

- Writing/mass communication
- Religion/spirituality
- Business development
- Music & art appreciation
- Sociological aspects of foreign cultures
- Nature and ecology
- Woodworking
- Sailing, skiing, running

RESUME PRIMER

After you have completed this exercise, you will write your resume (if appropriate). You may have a current resume, which you can use as a foundation to create a new, dynamic document more in tune with your Core Themes and the career direction you seek.

Your resume is your marketing document. It presents you to the marketplace (prospective employers). Remember, in most cases, employers will see your resume before they meet you. Therefore, before you submit your resume, think about how you want to be perceived by those reviewing it. What is the image you are trying to create in their eyes? It is important to create a resume that is relevant to the position for which you are applying. Experienced recruiters and human resources professionals can screen a resume in five to ten seconds. If they do not see skills and abilities that are relevant to the position, the resume goes into the "B pile," never to be seen again.

The fact that you are applying for a particular position or speaking with someone about a career opportunity suggests that you have done your homework on the company and the position and feel reasonably confident that they may be a good match for your Core Themes.

A logical place to incorporate some of your Core Themes is within the summary of qualifications statement that is the foundation of your resume. This statement, which usually appears at the top of a resume, should highlight your core abilities, interests, and skills as they relate to the position in question. For example, if one of your primary Core Themes is the need to work in a fast-paced, entrepreneurial business environment and this is consistent with the job description, then you would note this Core Theme with an example or two.

The important thing to remember as you network and apply for certain positions is to tweak and adapt your resume so that your core abilities and skills mesh with the position and the company's culture.

PLANNING YOUR CAREER SEARCH

Once your base resume has been completed, you will need to develop a career search plan. The actual plan will vary according to what you have learned about yourself through the Core Themes process. For example, you may want to pursue a career in marketing, or you have decided that owning your own business is a good match for your Core Themes and skills, or you may be considering returning to college to become a physician assistant, or you have discovered that you want to work in a nonprofit foundation that focuses on child poverty. Or you may not have a specific career in mind yet but want to explore a variety of career possibilities.

Regardless of which direction you choose, your Core Themes will guide you in analyzing and evaluating the myriad opportunities you uncover as you explore various options. For those who are pursuing their next career (not going to school or joining the family business), an important component of the plan is to create a list of people and businesses you can contact to learn more about the fields that interest you. Sarah and John are two examples of people who, guided by their Core Themes, found careers by exploring the options with people in the fields that interested them.

After Sarah quit her job—an unfulfilling position that left her feeling stressed and unhappy—she decided to take time to go through the Core Themes process before actively exploring other career opportunities. A few months later, armed with her Core Themes to guide her, relieved of stress and with renewed energy, she began her search for a new career. Consulting her list of networking contacts, she scheduled breakfast and lunch meetings to talk with people working in medical research, a topic that interested her. During the meetings, Sarah discussed her Core Themes experience and learned about new and fascinating careers in the field she had targeted. She found this experience energizing and refreshing, but most important, she discovered several career options she had not yet considered. In the course of these interviews, Sarah, a skilled writer, learned that research had shown that some women could alter the course of their cancer by changing their diet and adopting healthy eating habits. Intrigued, she interviewed a number of women who had successfully fought cancer through diet. When I met with Sarah, she announced with great excitement and enthusiasm that she had decided to write a book about the women who through dietary and other natural means had a positive impact on their cancer.

Sarah's experience is a common one with many of my Core Themes clients. In Phase 4 of the process (the Exploratory Phase), she had a general direction and interest but had not determined a specific career. Sarah was open to the possibilities as she networked with other people and learned about opportunities she had not explored before. Being open to the possibilities is key to the exploration phase.

In our work together, Sarah and I never really discussed the possibility that she would write a book or that she had any particular interest in cancer. When clients begin to let their Core Themes guide them in the exploration phase, what they discover often surprises them. Two of Sarah's Core Themes were innovation and intellectual stimulation. In her next career chapter, she wanted to be involved with people who would challenge and enlighten her. She said, "My work needs to make me think . . . and allow me to interact with people who are experts in their field." She was motivated to investigate innovative solutions and approaches. Most important, she was ready to take on new responsibilities and roles.

Sarah's newfound interest in women's cancer and the women who fought it through natural means stimulated her intellectual curiosity and her need to be challenged professionally and personally. It also provided the opportunity to satisfy her need for continuous learning.

Exploration can be an exciting experience, especially when you have your unique Core Themes to guide you.

John had been in retail management for most of his

professional career. After completing Phase 3 and developing a clearer picture of his Core Themes, he knew he did not want to return to managing people in a retail business. John's plan included the following considerations:

- He didn't want to be a retail manager.
- He was willing to travel but did not want to be away from his family for more than a day or two at a time.
- He wanted to be in a dynamic and growth-oriented company.
- He needed to earn a minimum of $80,000 a year with good health benefits.
- He needed to satisfy his number one Core Theme, his need for autonomy.
- He was open to all types of businesses: banking, retail, construction, technology, health care, and nonprofits.

John began networking aggressively, and in the course of eight weeks he met with more than sixty people from various businesses. He seriously considered buying a franchise but rejected this option after further investigation. An avid outdoorsman and skier, he applied for but didn't get a position teaching cross-country skiing to veterans with disabilities. Disappointed over his failure to win the job, he narrowed his focus. After an exhaustive networking effort, John landed a newly formed position with a successful and privately owned distribution company. In his new role, he was responsible for increasing the company's sales by working with customers to encourage them to expand their business with the company.

In his new role, John was able to meet all of his Core Themes while taking advantage of his years of retail management experience. One of John's endearing qualities is his ability to connect easily with people by building trust quickly. A likeable fellow, he exudes integrity and authenticity, a great asset that helped land his new job and is helping him win over his company's customers.

As you work your way through Phase 4, it is important to keep in mind your "must have" Core Themes as well as other factors such as income, benefits, travel requirements, and location of the company under consideration.

It is not always possible to find a job that will satisfy all of your Core Themes. That is why you have listed them in order of priority. Most of my clients find that if a job satisfies the top three or four of their Core Themes, they are happy with the new position. In most cases, the remaining Core Themes can be satisfied over time if one is patient. As we have stated before, your final decision also must take into consideration practical issues such as family needs, children's schooling, and personal lifestyle issues.

Lance's Core Themes centered around his artistic talents. After many years as a human resources professional, he discovered that he really wanted to spend his time painting images of his beloved Labrador retrievers. Lance had not been especially interested in art before, but the Core Themes process revealed his hidden dormant talents. Lance acknowledged, however, that being an artist would take time and training and probably would not bring in the high salary he was accustomed to in his current position.

With the full support of his wife, Lance set out to pursue his newfound love and joy. In the years since Lance opened his art studio, his life has changed dramatically. He supplements the income from his artwork by managing a successful pet business. Whether he is in his studio painting or managing the store, Lance's trusted black Labrador, Dillon, is by his side.

Lance has never looked back. Blessed with new friends

in the art world, he finds each day is filled with discovery and excitement as he creates innovative artistic designs and runs his own company. After changing his life and career course, Lance marvels at the transformation. "It's been years since I've felt this jazzed about what I'm doing," he said. "I feel in control of my own destiny. This feels right. I feel alive and excited about the future."

Using Core Themes and the Three Principles to Assess Career Options

As you consider the opportunities open to you, assess each one against the three principles for achieving true happiness and success discussed in Chapter 1. To review, these principles are as follows:

- Principle 1: You must love or at least like a lot the basic functions of the job you are engaged in day in and day out.
- Principle 2: You must respect and work well with other employees at the company.
- Principle 3: You must believe in the company's mission, values, and products or services, and approve of the way the company treats its employees. If you don't trust the leaders or respect the company, you are not going to be happy.

Let's say that one of your primary Core Themes is the need to use your strategic thinking abilities and skills. You are most fulfilled when you are involved in solving broad, complex business issues. After assessing a potential job against the three principles listed above, you may find that the work itself satisfies your Core Theme perfectly (Principle 1), but that most of your colleagues do not have the intellectual capabilities or the desire to assist you in your projects. Since that is the case, you may find it difficult to work with employees who do not share your abilities or work ethic (Principle 2).

Your assessment of Principle 3 suggests that the company and its leaders are a good match for your Core Theme. You judge the company to be progressive, innovative, and supportive of strategic and conceptual initiatives. So the potential job meets two out of three of the essential principles. Now you have to assess the risk of accepting a position, knowing that other employees may not meet your criteria.

In this hypothetical example, your primary Core Themes and the three principles help you come to a deliberate and objective decision on whether this job will work for you. If you choose to accept the position knowing that Principle 2 is lacking, at least you go into the job with your eyes wide open and with the knowledge that you may have to make adjustments to fulfill your responsibilities.

Many of my clients have found it beneficial to explain their Core Themes to prospective employers during the interview process. Employers are often impressed that candidates (my clients) have gone through a rigorous examination that has given them a clearer understanding of themselves as it relates to their career direction. The message to prospective employers is clear, that the candidates are not just looking for a "job" but are intent on securing a position that not only is compatible with their skills and experience but also matches their values, needs, and interests—their Core Themes.

Using your Core Themes combined with the success and happiness principles gives you the knowledge and confidence required to make informed and intelligent decisions about job opportunities. What a powerful tool!

Nine

Moving Forward
to Success and Happiness

*It is your life, and you alone control it. Your life is far
too valuable to waste. Now is the time to go forward
with purpose and meaning and live it well.*

Without a clear direction, we are likely to
flounder around for some time in pursuit of success
and happiness. Perhaps you will be one of the lucky ones
who stumble onto your dream career early in life. But do you
really want to leave one of life's most important decisions to
chance?

When asked how they chose their career, most of my
clients said that their career choice was not intentional, that
they had entered their profession by accident. For example,
one woman had an interest in fashion, so she studied at a
fashion institute and subsequently entered the retail business.
Now, many years later, she is a district manager responsible
for thirty retail stores. Her initial creative interests led her to

a job as a manager with responsibility for all aspects of store operations and the bottom line. Not a bad accomplishment; that is, if the position really makes her happy and fulfills her professionally and personally.

My clients often tell me that they chose their career path because they had a strong aptitude for a particular skill that then led them on a circuitous path to a job. For example, a person skilled in mathematical reasoning might go on to earn a degree in accounting, which then led them to a job as underwriter at a bank or a position in a public accounting firm. Or a young person with a passion for history might find herself years later stuck teaching History 101 for the umpteenth time to freshmen college students.

The influence of family and friends also can lead people to a particular career. When people you respect and love say you should go into law or medicine or become a teacher, it can be a strong motivator to choose a certain college and sign up for specific classes.

When you entered college at the age of eighteen, did you really understand the impact of your academic decisions on your life and future career for many years to come? When you are young and have no clue what you want to do for your life's work, you take the first good job offer that comes along. Perhaps a campus interview produced a job, or you landed in the retail food industry after applying for every job available. Now some twenty years later, you are a successful but far from happy store manager making a decent salary and feeling trapped. The clutter in your life is making it hard for you to seriously pursue another profession.

Not everyone who enters a career by accident is unhappy or unsuccessful. In fact, many of my clients whose careers were the result of chance enjoyed many happy and successful years in their jobs. But at some point they began to feel something was missing, and they became increasingly disenchanted with their jobs.

A key component of the Core Themes program is that people need to pursue happiness and success in life and in their careers both purposefully and deliberately. The chances of finding real success and happiness increase significantly when we know who we really are, what matters to us the most, and what we consider the true purpose of our life. Are we here just to take up space? Is there a greater purpose for our being? Regardless of your religious and spiritual beliefs, doesn't it make sense to live your life with a sense of purpose and meaning? Your Core Themes act as a guide or compass as you explore career opportunities. They make it possible for you to assess intentionally and deliberately whether a job is the best fit for you.

Let's examine how Martha relies on her primary Core Theme— analytical and conceptual ability—to set her criteria for a job. She determines that she needs

- to have a position in which she is able to focus on the task at hand and know that she will be given the opportunity to apply her best thinking;
- to be involved in big picture/strategic thinking—not day-to-day, tactical activities and duties;
- to be involved in a field that allows her to be intellectually stimulated and challenged; and
- to find an environment that respects and promotes quiet, introspective thinking and provides a peaceful, analytical atmosphere.

Mike follows a similar procedure. With a Core Theme that requires change, he knows he needs to work in a fast-paced environment. To be true to his Core Themes, he would choose to work in

- a company and a field that embrace change, ideally with change as a requirement for success; and
- a culture where he can execute changes successfully.

Both Martha and Mike had specific requirements of the jobs they eventually accepted. Thinking through these requirements carefully and evaluating the job based on their Core Themes gave them confidence that they had made the right choice. Of course, both Martha and Mike weighed all their Core Themes as well as the practical elements of the job such as salary, benefits, and other factors before making a decision.

By selecting jobs that are likely to satisfy their personal requirements, Martha and Mike have increased greatly their chances of achieving happiness and success in their careers.

Living A Meaningful Life

My Core Themes clients say their lives and careers are in much better balance when they follow their Core Themes. Using their Core Themes as a guide eliminates the guesswork when they have to make tough decisions about their jobs or personal lives. They simply follow their "personal compass," their unique Core Themes.

For the past three years Alicia has been on the journey of a lifetime in Africa. She is doing extraordinary work in Swaziland serving poor people and those afflicted with HIV. A role model for all young people, she is doing work that brings her great personal satisfaction and accomplishment.

Kim went from being a vice president of organizational development for a major food retailer to devoting much of her life to nonprofit organizations.

Jim has found his niche as a human resources professional for a manufacturing company in Seattle, where he is living his number one Core Theme of having the perfect balance of work and personal life.

If you embrace them, Core Themes will enrich and simplify your life. They will guide you in every major life and career decision you make. Like a compass, Core Themes will show you the way. Following your Core Themes can lead you to a life and a career full of meaning and purpose. But unlike a compass, they will not break or get lost. Core Themes are forever.

TEN

Tips for Finding
a Career Counselor

If you are reading this book, you are serious about finding a career that is personally and professionally rewarding. You may be a recent graduate in search of your dream job, a seasoned business professional who has become disenchanted with your career direction, a disillusioned attorney who has found the internal politics of your firm unbearable, a "burnt out" teacher who has lost the idealism and enthusiasm once so much a part of your career, or a nonprofit professional whose dream and passion to help others have been crushed by the bureaucratic complexity of the organization employing you.

Whatever your situation, you have come to a time in your life when you want to invest in understanding yourself and determining how to answer that most important question: "What do I want to do with my life?"

As we are often reminded, our time on this earth is limited. In recent memory we have experienced the loss of Steve

Jobs at the young age of fifty-six. Most likely you have experienced the loss of friends or family members who have died at a relatively young age.

Our time is precious and we should not take it for granted. It is finite! Your life isn't a dress rehearsal, it is the real deal. Why not choose a life and career that lead to happiness and success? Make it your number one priority!

In the following paragraphs, I have outlined a few of the factors to consider as you embark on locating a professional career counselor who can guide you in identifying your own unique Core Themes and finding true fulfillment in your career and life.

There are a number of professionals who provide career counseling services: career counselors, life coaches, life counselors, human resources consultants, and career consultants. A typical career counselor has a background in psychology, counseling, social work, sociology, human resources, or related field. That said, professionals who engage in career counseling may come from a number of disciplines including academia, law, medicine, business, financial consulting, and that of the professional trainer.

What to look for in a counselor:
Regardless of a counselor's academic background, it is important that he or she have a successful and substantial history of working with and helping people. The counselor must have an imbedded desire to help people, particularly those who are experiencing a serious transition. He or she ought to be well-versed in the various aspects of the world of business and the many opportunities available in both profit and nonprofit sectors.

The counselor also should have a general knowledge of

career and work-related opportunities within the educational field, technology, retail, science, religious and entrepreneurial tracks, law, engineering, accounting and finance, various businesses, and manufacturing.

The counselor ought to be a positive-thinking person, genuinely enthusiastic, mature, and emotionally stable, and possess excellent interpersonal skills. A high degree of empathy, emotional intelligence, and an unlimited supply of tolerance are a must.

Since the field is not regulated, professionals from various disciplines have "set up shop" and make claims that they have the expertise and knowledge to provide career-related services. In recent years, some people who themselves have had a transformation in their career believe that, because they made the transition, they now can help others. In some cases, this may be true, but be skeptical of seeing someone who does not possess a background in the behavioral sciences or who has not undergone serious training in career counseling. These people are well meaning but lack the depth of background in academics and experience to deal with serious career issues.

What questions to ask:
If you are serious about finding your true career direction, at the very least you should ask the following questions before making the commitment to work with a counselor:

- What is his/her background both academically and experientially?
- How did s/he get into the profession?
- Years of experience?
- Philosophy?
- Does s/he have a proven methodology? What is his/her standard approach to working with a client?

- Will s/he provide references?
- Does s/he use career/psychological tests, surveys, and questionnaires to assess clients' attributes, including personality profile, abilities, knowledge and experience, interests, aptitudes, emotional intelligence, and motivational profile?
- How does s/he handle sensitive emotional issues that you may be experiencing? (Most of my clients experience physical and emotional symptoms due to the stress of their jobs.)
- Does s/he have a website explaining his/her services and background in the field?
- Is s/he a life coach or a counselor?
- Will the counselor develop a plan and clarify the objectives of your program?
- Will the counselor involve your significant other, family members, or other loved ones in your assessment process?

I spend approximately twenty-four to thirty hours of office time with my Core Themes clients going through the program. Clients spend another twelve to fifteen hours on related "homework" (readings, writing, and other tasks). The entire process generally takes between two and three months to complete. Of course, the time required varies according to several factors: the severity of the person's unhappiness and stress, the age and level of maturity, the years of professional and life experiences (younger people have lived a shorter period of time and generally have less "baggage"), clients' level of commitment to the process and willingness to examine deeply and honestly their life and career, and other circumstances affecting the individual client.

A listing of professionals who have qualified to become official Core Themes counselors can be viewed by visiting the Core Themes website at www.corethemes.com. For useful books and other reference materials on finding the right career, please consult page 189 or visit the website.

ELEVEN

So You Want to Be
a Core Themes Consultant

Core Themes is a proven program that utilizes a unique methodology to help people of all ages and types find true passion and purpose in their career and life. *Core Themes are those unique, essential values, needs, and interests that define each of us personally and professionally.*

What are the benefits of becoming a licensed Core Themes consultant?
You will learn a unique, one-of-a-kind methodology developed over a seventeen-year period and proven to be effective with people from all walks of life. As a Core Themes consultant, you will

- become a more effective coach/consultant by establishing realistic data (based on objective results from more than thirteen tests, questionnaires, and the client's history) about your client's values, needs, interests, skills, abilities, and personal traits;

- build an action plan for your clients based on this data;
- develop a "road map" to true life/work fulfillment for your clients to follow and refer to anytime in their lives when they need to reexamine their choices;
- develop a coaching program for your clients based on scientifically determined data rather than on intuition, thus adding a valuable level of credibility to your work;
- deliver to your clients a prescribed four-phase program that generally takes about twenty hours of work with you (client will have about twelve hours of homework) and is delivered for a set price that the client knows in advance;
- offer clients a program with a defined time frame that is designed to be flexible and responsive to the client's current situation and needs; and
- provide clients with a program that takes the "whole" person into account.

As a Core Themes consultant, you will collect a comprehensive array of data about your clients, including:
- Motivational profile (underlying needs and motives)
- Emotional Intelligence
- Personal and professional values
- Personal profile
- Interest profile
- Abilities and aptitude profile
- Skills, knowledge, and experience assessment

What will be included in the training?
You will be enrolled in an intense five-day (and three eve-

nings) course preparing you to implement all four phases of the Core Themes methodology. During the course you will experience the Core Themes program firsthand and develop your own unique Core Themes. You will also learn how to

- qualify Core Themes clients
- assess clients and administer key tests
- interview clients to collect their unique personal and professional histories
- identify clients' "clutter" and help them manage or eliminate it
- assist clients in developing clarity about their purpose and direction
- build clients' personal and professional profile
- identify and evaluate clients' primary strengths and their limitations
- administer and interpret key written exercises completed by clients
- utilize various critical resources (books, movies, articles, and other materials)
- help clients create their own unique Core Themes
- develop a practical plan and strategy that enables clients to incorporate Core Themes in their careers and in their lives
- promote your business using our recommended business plan with a proven track record

What does the Core Themes license include?
- rights to use the copyrighted Core Themes methodology
- access to interpretations of test results by one of our qualified staff (including consultation on your individual clients' tests)

- listing on the Core Themes website
- referrals for potential clients in your area
- support services after completion of the training to answer questions that arise
- support materials (brochures and other promotional handouts)

Who can become a Core Themes consultant?

The Core Themes program has been developed to be used by professionals in the following fields:

- Executive coaches
- Career consultants/counselors
- Executive recruiters
- Life coaches
- Corporate coaches
- Human resources professionals
- Psychologists
- Licensed social workers
- Clinical therapists
- Management consultants
- Organizational management consultants

How do I get started?

For more information about Core Themes, visit our website at **www.corethemes.com**. For more information about licensing, contact Ray Inglesi, M.A. at e-mail: **ringlesi@corethemes.com** or by telephone at 1-866-353-3523 (local: 207-321-3523).

RESOURCES

Books

The Illustrated Alchemist by Paulo Coelho
Tuesdays With Morrie by Mitch Albom
Man's Search For Meaning by Viktor Frankl
Winners Never Cheat by Jon Huntsman
The Power of Myth by Joseph Campbell with Bill Moyers
The Age of Unreason by Charles Handy

Movies

The Mission, starring Robert De Niro
What the Bleep Do We Know!?

ACKNOWLEDGMENTS

I first got serious about writing this book several years ago. However, with a busy consulting practice and other commitments, I knew that it would be difficult to complete the project without help. This came in the way of a Core Themes client, Curt Hazlett, who had spent nearly twenty years in the newspaper industry, most recently as an editor for the *Portland Press Herald*. Curt and I met regularly for nearly a year. I talked and he wrote. The result was the beginning of what is now this book. I owe Curt a debt of gratitude. Without his patience and encouragement, I doubt this book would have been written.

I also owe a special thank you to Grace Noonan Kay, a respected colleague who for many years gently nudged me to write this book; to Ken Strait, a strong supporter of my work and a wonderful person; and to Peg Milardo for the many hours she spent proofing the final manuscript.

My deepest gratitude goes to my Core Themes clients, who opened their hearts and souls to the process. They have taught me much about what really matters in life and in one's career. Their willingness to share their innermost feelings, their fears, and their dreams has enriched this book and given it depth. I hope their stories will be an inspiration to others who are struggling to find purpose and meaning in their own careers. I am truly honored and blessed to have played a small part in the lives of so many of these wonderful people.

CPSIA information can be obtained
at www.ICGtesting.com
Printed in the USA
LVIW011204090712

289321LV00001B